THE PRIMACY EFFECT

To Mona

THE
PRIMACY
EFFECT

MICHAEL SHEA

 ORION
BUSINESS
BOOKS

The right of Michael Shea to be identified as the author of
this work has been asserted by him in accordance with the
Copyright, Designs and Patents Act 1988.

This edition first published in Great Britain in 1999 by
Orion Business
An imprint of The Orion Publishing Group Ltd
Orion House, 5 Upper St Martin's Lane, London WC2H 9EA

A CIP catalogue record for this book
is available from the British Library.

ISBN 0-75281-375-7

Typeset by Selwood Systems, Midsomer Norton
Printed and bound in Great Britain.

CONTENTS

Everyone sees what you appear to be: few experience what you really are.
Machiavelli

It ain't watcha say, it's the way howcha say it.
Louis Armstrong

First impressions are the most lasting.
Proverb

INTRODUCTION

I n the media-dominated environment in which we all live, a huge amount of attention is paid to image at the expense of substance. Reputations of people in the public eye are made or broken depending on how they seem – what the public perception of them is – rather than the underlying reality. Critics can carp and complain and say how unjust that all is, but it is exactly the same for the rest of us. What you are seen to be is what you are.

The *Primacy Effect* is the psychological term for the very first impression you make, or other people make on you. Research has shown how much more important and powerful that first experience is than any other single stimulus in establishing your short- and long-term reputation.

Style stifles substance. *Within the first fifteen seconds* of an applicant coming through the door, I have seen again and again how a negative Primacy Effect loses many of them that cherished job or promotion interview. Many candidates suffer from the naïve delusion that the facts about them as individuals, as set out in their carefully polished CVs and in their glowing reference letters, will somehow speak up for them unaided. They won't: background facts need a great deal of presentational help. The first step in that process is to appreciate how others immediately categorize and judge you when they don't know you.

This book builds on a great deal of psychological research and practical experience to explain how you can identify, present and communicate your own unique, personal selling point to others, reinforcing what nature has given you to advance your career. Life, after all, is about relationships. You go through your career being attracted to or repelled by other people, not, most of the time, on the basis of any deep or carefully considered knowledge of them, but on gut instinct, whether their faces appeal or not, and what their dress, bearing and expressions tell you about them. Initial, formative judgements are arrived at in an instant and are hard to shift. That is why you seldom get a second chance to make a favourable first impression.

Ill-delivered messages and badly chosen words can do a huge amount of damage in an instant. You see it in your private and public lives all the time, where, like it or not, style and visual image overwhelm the substance of your arguments. Public figures in commerce and industry are always being analysed, praised or torn apart by the media, which act like a primitive priesthood, creating gods, devils and clowns, roasting the self-important on their spits and otherwise dethroning the throned. Even if you are never going to be in the public eye you need to learn from this as well.

If you are interviewing others, despite what you may have heard about them from their referees, reports and CVs, you will still act largely on instinct. Everyone's tendency is to group, categorize or stereotype candidates; your judgements will largely be formulated on the basis of your previous experience of others who look, dress and sound like them. Consequently, many otherwise able and well-qualified individuals fail to get the recognition, the promotion or the high office they deserve, because they do not 'look the part', because they come across badly in interviews, or otherwise fail to communicate their strengths to those who have to assess them. For example, if there are three or four equally well-qualified candidates for a top position in industry, the professions or in the public sector, the successful one will almost certainly be the one who communicates best during the selection process and is judged as the one who will best 'fit in'. The television company GMTV was recently much criticized because its Director of Programmes was quoted as saying, on the subject of choosing presenters and newscasters, 'GMTV is about people looking attractive.' Possible stars, it was argued, had to have something called 'fanciability', or they did not get the job. Politically incorrect though that was widely held to be, the Director knew only too well the way things are: TV audiences switch on and stay switched on if they like the people they are watching, no matter what they say. We may not always realize it, but the rest of us react similarly in our day-to-day lives, switching on to those who appeal and ignoring or turning away from those who do not.

Communication Skills

While most people go on acquiring and improving their professional qualifications and gaining more and more skills throughout adulthood, after the age of five or six few make any attempt to improve the way they speak. Equally, spending too much time on your looks or the way you dress is seen as somewhat obsessive or as bad form. Otherwise highly intelligent and able people put little serious effort into trying to better their overall personal impact, advocacy and communication skills, and, to their detriment, ignore how crucial these skills are, not only to themselves but to the organizations they work in, lead or represent. Yet if they cannot perform well on their own account, they are hardly going to be able to do so for others.

Any film director knows that a meaningful look between two people on the screen can replace pages of script. Similarly, without a great deal of first-hand experience, the image or perception you have of someone, whether you have seen them on the silver screen, on TV or in reality, is generally the only thing you have to go on. In your turn, presentation skills, how you look, stand, dress and articulate, and how well you communicate with others, are key factors in seeking advancement. No matter how well you *think* you project yourself, your audience, be it one person or a thousand, is ruled by the sum of all these apparently trivial details.

A recent poll demonstrated that over 70 per cent of top managers and decision-takers, when asked what they most feared or disliked, admitted that it was having to speak in public or being interviewed live on radio or television. Many of them admitted openly that they communicate very badly indeed, even with their own colleagues, staff and customers, let alone with the outside world, yet few of them had made any serious attempt to improve. Even a day's professional personal communication training could have made all the difference.

Just as public reputations are made and broken on the television screen and in the pages of the newspapers more than in the committee rooms and offices in which such important people operate, so it is with the rest of us. You may be good at what you do, but unless you are recognized as being good, you are, at best, ignored. If you have any ambition, you need to spend much more time thinking about the health of your reputation. If it is less than robust, the personal spin-doctoring techniques set out throughout this book will help greatly.

Laurence Olivier may have been cynical when he said, 'If you can fake sincerity, you can fake anything', but unless you realize how important it is to be well perceived by others and recognize what you *can* do to improve your public image, you lose out. That is just common sense. Casting directors pick and choose actors to play roles all the time. Of course you have to be sincere, genuine and honest, but to get your point across more professionally you have a role to play as well. You can improve, easily and dramatically.

This book is about how to go about it. It is not about creating some fantasy façade around yourself, making you into something you are not, but about building up and strengthening the reality. Drawing on what psychologists and psychiatrists have discovered about how each and every one of us reacts to new people, it sets out to show you how you can recognize and develop your communication skills more effectively and, by so doing, improve that immediate rapport, the Primacy Effect, also known as the Law of Primacy or the Principle of Primacy, you have on others.

To begin with you have, with as much detachment as you can muster, to admit to and analyse why people, in varying but often highly undramatic ways, take to or against you. Most people are frightened of confronting this basic issue frankly. You then have to move on to use your upside attributes and downplay or eliminate your downside elements, in order to gain more out of your business and social life. To repeat: this book does not attempt to turn you into something that you are not, by inventing some sort of new persona for you, but to help you recognize how you can better exercise your existing presentational skills.

Many people consider themselves so much in control of their own destinies that they don't need to pick up a self-help book such as this and never think of seeking or accepting professional advice on how to package and present themselves better. They are of the 'I get on OK' or the 'take me the way I am' school. They are among the ones who, despite being intelligent and highly skilled, fail to recognize, or bury deep inside themselves, even rather startling social and professional defects and inadequacies. Serious downside characteristics are marginalized by them as they stumble through life. Ill-thought-out ways of speaking, ingrained personal habits or a scruffy, insanitary appearance have sunk many a career, leaving the individual concerned flailing around looking for others to blame, when the problem could so easily have been remedied. We all know people who have become failures largely owing to such trivial details. It is not just princes, prime ministers and pop stars who need image consultants to put them on the right track. The rest, those of you who are not prepared to have your ambitions thwarted and don't suffer from the arrogant belief that you can do without advice, will find that this book lists the key areas where much of the trouble often lies in your daily attempts to advance towards a more profitable and agreeable way of life.

Who stands out in a crowd and why?

To highlight some of these points right at the outset, ask yourself the following very basic questions:

1. Why, in a room full of strangers (setting aside sexual attraction), do you find that some people stand out?
2. Does how people look affect your judgement of them? Are you sure?
3. Why do some people, even those not in senior positions, get listened to much more than others?
4. Why do some people, as soon as they appear or open their mouths, immediately get, to use an American expression, 'negatively defined'?
5. Are you good at communicating? Do people listen to you? What are your negative points? What are you going to do to rectify them?

Throughout your life you continually try to improve on many fronts, even if it is only cooking a tastier soufflé or reducing your golf handicap. Why therefore not spend just that little bit more time in improving how you look, stand, inspire confidence, and, above all, say what you say to other people? There is no one set of invariable rules for all this, but the guidelines are all here.

Universities and business schools create fictional, though highly 'real', case studies to help as teaching aids. In a modest way, this book follows suit. It includes a number of imaginary but realistic conversations and case studies, drawn from actual business- or work-related examples, which help to highlight the essential issues and offer solutions to the most common problems people meet when trying to present themselves and their ideas in a more compelling way. While the spin-doctors of political life have had a rather bad press recently, rather like a personal trainer in a health club, a personal spin-doctor can show you the best practice for promoting yourself and your ambitions more effectively.

I have used a fair number of world-famous politicians and other international figures to exemplify what to do and what not to do because their presentational antics and successes will be more familiar to more readers of this book, than if I had taken all my examples from any particular country's business or commercial life. There are also many quotations in this book. I make no apologies for being a burglar of other people's words, since they benefit from further recognition and display. These quotes – look, for example, at the very last one in the book – show that men and women across the ages have always recognized the importance of communicating well in public, and of improving their personal impact generally.

Bill, the Senior Manager, paced nervously up and down outside the Chairman's office. What the hell did JD want this time? He was always having bees in his bonnet about one thing or another. After a few minutes the buzzer sounded.

'Morning, JD,' Bill said confidently, as he entered the room. He liked to think he came across well. There was no beating about the bush with him. A spade was always...

'Morning, Bill,' said the Chairman drily. He did not get up from his desk. 'Been thinking. The company needs fresh outside help.'

'Absolutely, JD,' said Bill. 'New strategic line-up, eh? My views entirely.'

'No, Bill . . . Communicating. We're bad at it.'

'Quite right, JD. Never thought our PR department was up to much. And as for our in-house magazine . . .'

'Not talking about that either, Bill. I'm talking about image. Presence. The way our senior people communicate . . .'

'I'll draw up a list of outside PR companies, JD. Organize a beauty parade. They can do a pitch and I'll put the best one up to you,' volunteered Bill brightly.

'I'm ahead of the game on this one too, Bill,' said the Chairman. Only then did Bill become aware of another person in the Chairman's office. A woman, her back to him, was pouring a cup of coffee at a side table. She turned and smiled sweetly at him. She was obviously JD's new PA. He was always changing them.

'Milk and sugar?' the woman asked pleasantly.

'As I was saying,' the Chairman interrupted, 'I'm engaging a company spin-doctor.'

'Smart idea, Boss. Spin-doctor, eh? Up with the times. As I said, I'll identify a key player and have him pitch to us and then . . .'

'This spin-doctor is specifically going to look at how *you* could communicate better. I have high hopes of you, Bill, grooming you for stardom and so on. But there are one or two rough edges . . .'

'Me?' Bill smiled a forced, self-satisfied smile. 'But I'm known . . . Look you've got to be . . .' Something on the Chairman's face caused him to pause.

'Sure thing, JD,' he said, backing off. 'We can all do with a bit of a polish.' He turned, nodded absent-mindedly in the direction of the woman, sipping at the cup of coffee she had given him. Cool chick. He might try chatting her up later. Nice pair of legs there.

After a moment, he regained his natural bravado. 'So what will this spin-doctor guy teach me that I can't do on my own?' asked Bill. Absurd. Everyone knew he was the best of after-dinner speakers, the funniest teller of jokes . . . the all-round great guy . . .

'For a start, she won't let you jump to premature conclusions, Bill. Let me introduce you to Dr Ruth Mackenzie.' The Chairman turned to the woman, who stretched out her hand in greeting. Despite himself, Bill had the decency to blush.

CHAPTER 1

The Mask and the Man

How we 'read' and pigeon-hole other people

The minute you walked in the joint,
I could see you were a man of distinction,
A real big spender.
Good looking, so refined,
Say, wouldn't you like to know what's going on in my mind?
'Big Spender', 1966 song

Men in general judge more from appearances than from reality.
All men have eyes, but few have the gift of penetration.
Machiavelli

Things are seldom what they seem,
Skim milk masquerades as cream.
W. S. Gilbert, HMS Pinafore

Understanding the Primacy Effect in the highly competitive world of the twenty-first century is going to be as crucial as any tool you use for your personal advancement. Your visible profile has to be polished to perfection in this age of instant communications where so many people and ideas are competing for the available attention.

Precisely why do people react in the way they do to the first sight of others, their accents, their dress, their appearance? Some immediately attract us, some bore us, a few repel. Once we know some of those answers, we can then condition ourselves to being more instantly acceptable to others. This is not as obvious a statement as it seems. *Recognition* rules the game.

Magritte, the Belgian surrealist artist, once painted a smoker's pipe on a canvas with the title 'Ceci n'est pas une pipe', meaning 'This is not a pipe'. He was right: it was not a pipe. It was only a picture of a pipe on canvas. But in our mind's eye it was still a pipe. For most of us for most of the time, the picture we have of something or someone is the only aspect we consider.

The British are said to take pride in camouflaging their true nature by *not* letting their feelings show. An outpouring of emotion, especially in public but also in private life, is just not on. Yet we all spend an inordinate amount of time trying to overcome this barrier by attempting to read what others are thinking, and seeing if we can guess what their true reactions to us and our ideas are likely to be. What we glean from their expression is often all the evidence we have, particularly if we have never met them or had other experience or report of them in the past. How we react to them will be based on this flimsiest of information, yet that first reaction to them, and of them to us, rules our future relationship, whether positively or negatively, until some other major experience comes along to interfere with it. We don't consciously think about any of this very much since our lives are too busy to be deeply judgemental every time we meet someone. Usually that doesn't matter; sometimes it matters very much indeed.

Some people exude sincerity, others patently do not. Sounding credible or believable is enormously important. The integrity of people like Mo Mowlam, the UK government's Northern Ireland Secretary, shines through every time she appears on the television screen. She looks incapable of saying anything other than what she sincerely believes. It is not that her predecessor, Sir Patrick Mayhew was insincere, but his patrician, high Tory manner of speaking gave an impression of loftiness and disdain which many Irish men and women of various persuasions found difficult to tolerate. The manner of the man overrode the content of his messages in this crucial arena.

Try looking more closely at the question of instant perception as it affects you. When you are next in any pub, club, office or organization to which you belong to or to which you go daily, have a look around you. If you are describing to others your colleagues Smith, Brown or Jones, how many adjectives do you allow them? Each is a highly complex individual. But do you categorize them in your own mind with more than one or two shorthand words? You will almost certainly have them branded as hardworking, dependable, flamboyant, timid, tedious, thoughtful or thoughtless. They are weighed up very briefly, and then, unless you have a great deal of subsequent exposure to them, they are pigeon-holed away in the recesses of your mind.

The Branding of Individuals

In a similar, simplistic way, we tend to sum up major public figures whom we see only on our television screens. Often such individuals' reputations are tied to or branded by a single incident which, from then on, encapsulates all that they are and stand for. Boris Yeltsin, for example, has been branded as something of a buffoon for dancing drunkenly in full view of the TV cameras, an impression enhanced by his non-appearance on a stop-over from New York to Moscow in the Republic of Ireland, because he was dead drunk, or had had a slight stroke. Though the rest of the world tended to mock him, the Western democracies supported him as being the least unstable of the current band of Russian leaders. Above all, his slurred speech after his heart attack, even if one did not understand a word of Russian, spoke volumes to us all.

Similarly, any Western politician will be perceived as clever, stupid, good, bad, colourful or boring, when he or she has a huge range

What does this picture say about character?

of complex characteristics which we have neither the time nor the inclination to recognize. Former UK Prime Minister John Major, for example, was always seen, even by his opponents, as an honest and honourable man, but the public perception of him was of a grey, passionless figure, who had an inability to bridge the barrier between the language he used and the lifeless way he delivered it. To demonstrate political impartiality, I should also quote what the veteran British Labour politician Roy Hattersley said about the present UK government's Minister without Portfolio and spin-doctor supreme: 'If Peter Mandelson is such a genius at image-building, how come his own image makes even his friends squirm?'

One-adjective descriptions of people are particularly clearly symbolized in the cartoon trade. Good cartoonists will pick out one outstanding feature of their victim – Prince Charles's ears, John Major's dominant upper lip, Tony Blair's staring eyes – to illustrate their man or woman. The *Spitting Image* puppet-makers picked up and exaggerated that one particular attribute – big nose, weak chin, or whatever – and, fairly or unfairly, used it to brand or lampoon the person concerned.

Picture editors of newspapers are similarly adept at choosing the right simplistic image to back up a story. If a Captain of Industry is said to be furious about something, they will scour the depths of their picture libraries to find one which has the individual concerned looking as angry as possible. When they decide someone is to be a love or a hate figure, they will dig up the appropriate shot, and the fact that it may have been taken in different circumstances at a totally different time and place will not stop it being used to influence the public mind.

A splendid case of dog eating dog in the media occurred recently when a photograph of Rupert Murdoch looking extremely worried and downcast was widely used – in papers which he did not own – to illustrate his announcement of a dramatic fall in News Corporation's annual profits.

It is not dissimilar with us lesser mortals. Despite the fact that it is no more logical than to judge a movie by looking only at the blow-up of the opening frame, the first image you present to someone sticks and sticks hard.

How We Read What We See

Look in more detail at how we 'read' other people. We are conditioned by birth and upbringing in the way we react to specific individuals and events. No matter how liberal and enlightened we believe we are, some people naturally attract us because of their backgrounds, education, race, looks, habits and attitudes, just as we can be fiercely repelled by others. Sometimes such reactions are justified by some personal experience we have had; sometimes we are totally and absolutely unjust and are merely demonstrating our own prejudices.

Our eyes take in only a tiny part of the evidence when we see a man or woman across a crowded room, or of what we could observe while we are walking to the office. We draw certain conclusions from what we think we have recognized about someone. But that scruffy workman digging up the street at our feet could in fact be a nuclear scientist fallen on hard times, just as the brains of the sensational but empty-looking catwalk model could actually match her looks. Our minds are at times overwhelmed and at times lazy; they read only what they feel they need to read about what they see, interpreting that view to our consciousness in a similar shorthand form. In other words, most of us are not very good at paying attention to what does not interest or concern us, including what other people are saying, unless we like them, or want to please them, or to benefit ourselves by the information they are imparting. In all life, there are certain reactive keys that invigorate us, and others that are on permanent switch-off.

When we walk down a street there are literally millions of things to see, but we filter out a massive majority of them to concentrate on what attracts our attention or what we believe is essential to our well-being. Our various senses – sight, hearing, touch, smell – are in a continuous state of activity or flux. All is out there to be analysed or retrieved, but, in practice, very little of it is allowed in through our in-built self-protective filters. In physical terms, this contact with the world around us is a very sophisticated process of physical energy stimulating our various sensory organs – sound waves to our ears, light for our vision and so on – information that is then processed and interpreted by our brain, which is conditioned to react in certain ways to the data received. We experience an agreeable reaction to a beautiful view, an artistic masterpiece, a great film, a piece of jewellery, a pretty baby or whatever, but we will recoil with terror at meeting a man brandishing a handgun. Most of the time our habit, out of necessity, is simply to ignore most of what else is going on out there. What we do allow in, we automatically assemble, analyse and sort on our internal database. The brain divides up its tasks, winnowing out the chaff, and keeping what it thinks is the crucial seed, the most prom-inent features of people and objects. Thus, in a theatre audience of hundreds, a man will notice a devastatingly pretty girl, for example, while foolishly ignoring dozens of others who might suit his social or aspirational circumstances very much better. Similarly at a job interview, as we shall see, one person will be chosen and others discarded on the basis of some specific, often trivial, stimulus or characteristic.

We are also conditioned to interpret certain signs and signals in certain ways. If a man laughs, we believe him to be amused. If he scowls, he is angry. We look through the windows that are our senses, keeping out and letting in only what we choose, a selection process based largely on our memory of similar previous experiences and what our subsequent expectancies of them are. When they first appeared on our Western television screens, the figures who emerged from behind the old Iron Curtain, notably Lech Walesa, the Polish Trade Union leader with his big moustache, his flamboyant style and his smile, and then Mikhail Gorbachev, who also smiled and appeared human, gave a whole new impression to the Kremlin watchers, conditioned by years of seeing only grim political leaders of the 'Evil Empire'. These new leaders not only smiled, they seemed to be interested in other people, they waved to the crowds genuinely, not with the mechanical gestures of those who used to stand watching the massed ranks of Russian troops march past Lenin's tomb. By so doing – and here is a splendid international example of the Primacy Effect – they totally changed the perception of what was going on in the Soviet Union, and that perception alone hastened the eventual fall of the Iron Curtain.

To See Ourselves . . .

There is no simple 'absolute truth' about another person, any more than there is about ourselves. The laughing man may be about to hit us. We are all hugely complex individuals, but we still retreat to using shorthand when we talk about 'the real him' or 'the real me' and so on. If we are at all introspective, we look at ourselves in a mirror and think we are being objective in analysing what we see, while it cannot ever really be the case. We employ terms such as being 'self-conscious' (usually used to described shyness, but it has a deeper meaning) or 'self-aware', but that can really only be a partial picture of what everyone else sees. There are a hundred other ways of defining the picture we have of ourselves – ego, identity, self-concept, self-image, self-regard – but trying to answer with any precision the questions 'Who am I?', 'What am I?' and 'What worth have I?' is totally bewildering to almost all of us. As we will see from the Case Study at the end of this chapter, every personality trait we have is a matter of judgement and opinion even among those who know us well. In the end we can really only be defined in comparison with other people, and all the characteristics we think we possess can only be judged in relation to similar attributes of those around us.

Bill, the Senior Manager, in his chauvinistic, thick-skinned way rapidly got over his initial embarrassment at mistaking Dr Ruth Mackenzie for the Chairman's new secretary. But the incident had reinforced his prejudice that this so-called spin-doctor woman was someone neither he nor the company needed. It was all gimmicky. Spin-doctors were for political parties, not for serious business organizations, let alone for him. As if he needed spin-doctoring! There was absolutely nothing wrong with his presentational skills. Look how well he had done in life.

He was, however, perfectly polite, if somewhat distant, when they had their first face-to-face meeting. It took place in his office, with the barrier of his executive desk between them.

'So,' he said rather too loudly, 'not much wrong with this company, I think you'll find. The bottom-line figures look pretty good this year. Business is booming and the market is racing ahead.'

'What about the competition?' asked Dr Mackenzie, softly.

'Sure, they get a good press,' said Bill, 'but it don't bother me. Profit is the only thing that matters.'

'What about your own reputation?'

Bill shrugged. 'Truth game, eh? OK, I'll play. People have to take us – me – the way I am,' he said, wishing she would go away. He had real work to do.

'And what way are you?' she asked, with the slightest smile.

A trifle self-consciously, Bill straightened his tie. 'I believe in dressing smart, being smart, talking straight. No bullshit.'

'Good on you. But that tie, for example,' said Dr Mackenzie.

'Tie? What about it? An old girlfriend bought it for me.'

'That shows a great deal of loyalty.'

'Hey, are you getting personal?' Bill started getting aggressive.

'Do you want to hear or don't you?'

'What about? About me?' asked Bill. 'OK, go ahead, I can take it. I don't believe in all this spin mumbo jumbo. But what JD says goes.' He sat back in his chair, self-confident and complacent.

'Right,' said Dr Mackenzie. 'My first impression of you was far from positive, but in time we'll get over that hurdle. I'll admit to one thing though: I typecast or pigeon-holed you as you did me.'

'What d'ya mean?' said Bill. 'Me a type? I'm a one-off.'

'You may well be . . . probably are. We all are in a way, but it doesn't stop us briefly categorizing each other and putting the results into separate little boxes. Yours, if you don't mind me saying, is labelled "successful, aggressive male".' Bill smiled a tight-lipped smile as she continued. 'You know, it's not just job interviews that are won or lost within the first fifteen seconds of coming through a door. Unless people have a positive image of you, they're not going to listen to you and certainly not going to agree to your strategy proposals, no matter how sound they are, if they don't like you in the first place.'

'You're right there. Have you met Rawlings in Sales? He's a pain. I switch off as soon as he opens his mouth. But as for me, people respect me, I think. In any case, to hell, they'll have to take me as I am,' said Bill, a fraction grumpily. 'Or lump it.'

'Quite right. But what I am here to do, Bill, like it or not, is to make sure you understand that there may be a downside risk to you in how people see you. At a guess there's a lot of in-built negative in your reputation as well as positive.'

Bill shrugged again. 'Go ahead. Pile it on. I can take it.'

As Brecht said in the *Threepenny Opera*: If you pass a one-armed beggar, on the first day you may give him a pound, on the second you may give him half that, but the third time you see him, you call the police to get him off your doorstep. We react differently to things as we gain experience of them. We cannot totally divorce ourselves from physical considerations, even if we think we do. We all react differently to different stimuli. One man's choice of ties or his table manners may be anathema to us and affect our relationship with him. But subjectively it may also tell us something about him. Colleagues may smile at us when we meet them, but if the smile is only on the lips and not in the eyes, they may appear insincere, leading us not to trust them or their arguments. If a person has some quality that is not fully recognized or at least sensed by us, either because it is concealed or because it does not attract our attention in some way, then it might as well not exist. We can never be totally objective in our judgements. To be fair, if we were, we would become completely overwhelmed by the amount of facts and sensations and details that always surround us. This gives us an immediate clue as to how important it is, if we want to impress someone at an interview or elsewhere, to send out clear and unambiguous signals which are certain to be both noticed and read correctly by those sitting across the green baize table from us. We have to learn to capitalize on the fact that those other people are just as selective as we are in what they take in, and that they will infer much more as well as much less than is justified about us from the information and impression we present them with.

Everyone conceptualizes, extrapolates and draws conclusions that are way beyond what such surface information should justify. When we see a man smiling at us, we assume that he is not going to harm us and that he is going to be friendly, whereas this may be far from the truth. We see a car driving along a road and presume that it is going from A to B when in fact it may be about to do a U-turn. We see a woman carrying a suitcase and presume that it's hers. There are lots of much more subtle circumstances in everyday life which lead us to instantaneous judgements about people and activities which are not justified by the amount of evidence we have in front of us.

The Halo Effect

Take physical appearance, for example. It may be grossly unfair, but how a person looks particularly determines our judgement of them. Think of Arnold Schwarzenegger! It is like coming across a beautiful rose: it *looks* nice, therefore it must smell nice. This cross-branding with regard to people, sometimes referred to by psychologists as the *Halo Effect*, causes someone handsome or attractive like, say, Harrison Ford, who looks trustworthy, sincere and so on, to be assumed also to be wise, competent and gifted in other ways, even though we have absolutely no reason whatsoever for making such assumptions. Other common examples abound, where appearance and character are auto-matically bound up with each other. A man with a high forehead wearing horn-rimmed glasses will tend to be thought of as highly intelligent, and a fat man as jolly, just as a woman who is too good-looking, dresses very fashionably and wears a lot of make-up can all too easily be branded as vain, snobbish or even flighty. We are usually totally unaware that we are subconsciously and instantaneously making other such judgements. For example, if an individual has physical or behavioural traits that we do not find attractive, he or she will be unfairly damned by us because of the implicit assumptions we make that they will probably have numerous negative characteristics in addition.

Beauty and the Primacy/Halo Effect brings other baggage with it as well. Would the violinist Vanessa Mae be quite so popular and get quite the attention she does purely for her performing skills if she were not also a beauty? Would the intelligent and able former President of the Irish Republic, Mary Robinson, have made such an international impression if her kindness and warmth and good looks had not been so totally apparent? Would Aung Sam Suu Kyi, the Burmese Nobel Peace Prize winner, get quite so much world attention, if she too were not stunningly charming and serene? There is no doubt that she is a very brave and intelligent woman who has suffered many years of house imprisonment, but the fact of the matter is that beauty imprisoned, ever since the days of St George and the Dragon, has always given a highly appealing tug on the world's heartstrings.

The Primacy/Halo Effect spreads into every area of activity. Like Tiger Woods, the English tennis ace Tim Henman, because of his boyish good looks and the fact that he is not a spoilt brat like so many others on the international circuit, attracts to himself the reputation of being an all-round good guy in the eyes of his fans. Another sporting hero, Frank Bruno, can move from boxing ring to theatre stage and make the world enjoy his antics.

Sometimes we are badly caught out by all this. When Radovan Karadzic, the former leader of the Serbs, later a indicted war criminal, started appearing on television, he was given a fair hearing. With his unruly, grey head of hair, he looked interesting and rather like a prosperous Western businessman. By contrast, his equally unpleasant army colleague, Ratko Mladic, always appeared at the Serbian stronghold at Pale looking like an out-and-out thug. Again, one does not need to look powerful to be so. By contrast with people like these, the modest and bespectacled US envoy to Bosnia, Richard Holbrooke, looked positively unassuming, yet had a huge underlying tenacity and determination, as does that other US mediator, the equally unassuming, bespectacled and modest Dennis Ross, who has, for the past five years, been shrewdly trying to bring about a Middle East peace settlement.

Not all of us can be blessed with good looks, however, and those who are not can still win through by dint of personality. No one would ever accuse David Bellamy or David Mellor of being conventionally handsome, but it didn't stop either of them from reaching the top of his particular tree. Mikhail Gorbachev, meanwhile, with that famous birthmark across the front of his forehead, was even said to have been driven by this grit-in-the-oyster factor to carry out his epoch-making role.

People Like Us

Without getting embroiled in psychological detail, you need to accept that other people seldom break up their perceptions of you into parts, unless they know you very well and come to recognize you as a highly complex, composite being. You will, as I said above, be branded on first sight as a stereotype creature who is good, bad, efficient, sloppy or whatever. Subjectively, much of this depends on their and your own emotional and personal background. To take an extreme case, if, as a child, you were once frightened by a man with a big black beard, then this may, when such a person comes in front of you in your position as Head of a Personnel Department, make you less likely to offer him a job.

Psychologists have developed a number of related theories about how we recognize and react to historically based factors in coming to a packaged judgement about our fellow men and women. It is sometimes referred to as *Pattern Recognition*, a system of analysing our responses in terms of 'template matching', that is, relating the person we see in front of us now to similar people we have come across in the past. If someone new swims into our ken who reminds us of someone who is terribly efficient, that new acquaintance will be imbued with similar characteristics until they prove otherwise. The image of O. J. Simpson was of the all-American hero who looked good, sounded good and epitomized all that was best in black American society. Here was a superhero, and large numbers of people felt they could look up to him. Everyone wanted to like him because he was big and strong and successful and agreeable looking. Then the worst happened and the rest is history.

Just as we know we will be burned if we put our hand in a fire or that drinking a glass of water will quench our thirst, we make automatic judgements based on all sorts of memories and experiences – both short- and long-term – and filter this through the same automatic retrieval process I discussed earlier. This is sometimes called *Prototype Theory*, which, as its name suggests, is where we again react to a given set of personality stimuli (blue eyes and blond hair suggest Nordic origins and swarthy dark skin that someone is of Mediterranean origin) to make a range of other judgements about them. Just as we recognize written words that are made up from letters of the alphabet, so we configure facial and body features and then 'read' what we think we see, reacting to certain cues or memory clues, stripping away any extraneous information in the process.

Time and Place

In coming to a judgement on someone, much depends as well on *the context* in which we meet them. A man or woman encountered at a

How many attitudes and judgements are in play here?

late-night party may be highly appealing then, but seen in a distressingly different light the next morning. A businessman may be highly competent at running a company when things are going well, but may, like many of us, give a very different, negative impression when he is seen coping with a crisis or conflict situation.

Even today, when companies no longer insist on very strict dress codes for all their employees, we still see evidence of conformity or lack of it in what people wear. Identikit men and women, often dressed in the same pinstriped suiting, carrying the same briefcases and computer bags, and beneficiaries of the same well-sprayed hairdos, are marked out as company men and women. How do any of them stand out as individuals unless we see them off duty or at play? We spend a lot of time trying to distinguish them from one another in order to gauge how we think they are going to behave or react in any given set of circumstances. Before we choose to employ Mr X as Finance Director, we want to know whether he will be able to serve the company well both in good times and in bad. So we test him by setting him in different contextual conditions. We try to predict or anticipate his actions, largely on the basis of previous experience of him. If we have never come across him before, the guessing game becomes harder, and we have to infer things beyond the mere 'facts' about Mr X as they are presented to us.

Much of our judgement about other people perforce relies also on second-hand information. We attribute characteristics and behaviour patterns to someone as a result of hearsay, even though we do not know the circumstances in which he or she acted in a certain way. To be told, for example, that someone 'panics' will suggest a serious weakness unless we are also informed that the specific panic was brought about by his house having been burned down around him. Equally, if we are told that someone is an extrovert, we will be preconditioned to expect someone whom we have stereotyped as being sociable, bubbly and easy to get on with. Thus you have always to be alert to the fact that former colleagues and employers can set up an image of you long before you even walk through the door. No matter how good your Primacy Effect is when you appear in a new setting, it will have been coloured, for good or bad, by the letters, reports, gossip or whispers of others. Generally, there is little, even if you know it is going on, that you can do about all that, except rise above it and prove yourself in an immediate, first-hand way.

Whether or not you are convinced yet that your Primacy Effect is critical to your standing, there is no doubt, as I said above, that we are all sometimes led seriously astray by first impressions. Lord King and his senior colleagues at British Airways are on record as saying that if Richard Branson of Virgin Airways, when he started challenging their supremacy on the transatlantic routes, had appeared at their meetings dressed in a more conventional style in a suit and tie, clean shaven and wearing horn-rimmed glasses, then they might have taken him seriously from the outset. Equally, Bill Gates himself says that people tended to dismiss him at first because he looked 'a bit goofy'. Churchill and Chamberlain shared one thing in common: they both at first thought that Adolf Hitler was an absurd-looking little fellow with a stupid little black moustache and slicked-down hair, who preened and postured around in a way that neither of them took particularly seriously. The legendary Chancellor of modern Germany, Helmut Kohl, with his energy and cunning, has held on to power longer than most post-war European leaders. His pre-eminent position in Europe, as far as his reputation is concerned, is partly to do with the fact that in all the group photographs of the European Community leaders, he towered in bulk and height above all the dwarves that stood around him. His long shelf-life also meant that he was always there while others came and went, leaving him perceived throughout the world to be *the* European leader above all. Within Germany, meanwhile, he was adept at side-stepping the blame for many of the country's economic and political misfortunes, leaving it to colleagues such as Theo Weigel, the Finance Minister, to act as scapegoats for the German government's difficulties.

In sum, we are all highly selective in the attention we give to others, not out of sloppiness but because of what we have been told and, more basically, because there are neurological limits to what we can ever assimilate. There is an automatic bottleneck which filters out the unnecessary and the unwanted, as when you go to a noisy cocktail party or enter a crowded pub. You *hear* a huge amount of noise, laughter, chatter or music, but you only *listen* to what you need or wish to hear. You accept only that which is *pertinent* to you, owing to the limits you have to your processing capacities. In everyday life you ignore this simple truth at your peril.

Why the hell had JD, when he'd gone off the top on this, chosen a woman as a so-called spin-doctor? It was just adding to the aggro. Apart from riling him as she already had – or was it a wind-up? – what the devil could she teach him that ...? He suppressed his irritation, summoned up courage, and raised his concerns with the Chairman.

The latter was blunt. 'First of all, Bill, over half of our customers, our employees, and the media people we have to deal with, even a good percentage of our shareholders – are women. The female viewpoint is important. And besides, Bill ... She's the best...'

'But ...' Bill began, the wind taken from his sails.

'If you have serious concerns, just let me know, Bill,' said the Chairman firmly. 'I could always put her together with young Stevenson. He's got a lot of potential, don't you think?' He looked away and waited.

'It'll be a real pleasure working with Miss, er ... Dr Mackenzie, JD. You know me: I love challenges,' Bill said as he stood up. They both smiled at each other, reading their mutual lack of sincerity, then Bill left the room.

'People get to know me in due course,' said Bill to Dr Mackenzie with forced geniality some time later. 'They judge me as I am.' He resolved to work hard on her.

'In due course is too long a time for most interpersonal situations,' replied Ruth Mackenzie firmly. 'The first impact you make is key. But let's start at the beginning: if you stand up and address the employees here, what d'you think they think of you?'

'Pretty good ... I hope ...' he hesitated. 'In any case I don't care. All I expect of them is that they do what they're told.'

'Sure. I'm not suggesting that as a boss you want to make them love you,' she said patiently. 'But don't you think they might work better for you if they respected you?'

'They do respect me.'

'How d'you know?'

There was a long silence. 'Well I'm certainly not going to bloody well ask them.'

'Of course not,' she said, soberly, 'but there are other ways of finding out. If you're prepared to see this through and work with me, why don't you start by telling me truthfully how you think other people see you?'

'Good opening gimmick,' said Bill, keeping his irritation in check. 'But no. *You* do the work. Tell me how *you* see me – warts and all.'

He smiled what he thought was a devastating smile. Then, equally suddenly, he had a twinge of doubt that his renowned charm with the ladies wasn't quite working the way it should.

SELF-ASSESSMENT AND ASSESSMENT EXERCISE

PERSONAL AND CONFIDENTIAL

JOB SPECIFICATION

The subject is a Senior Manager (Sales) of a small computer company. The market is tough and the competition intense.

CANDIDATE'S SELF-ASSESSMENT

I have been in the job for a year. I find the work challenging and rewarding, though the hours are long and I would prefer to have more assistance. I travel a great deal, perhaps four days out of five.

I am highly self-motivated and am always looking for new market opportunities. I believe I work well under pressure. My strategic thinking is good and my time/diary management is, I believe, above criticism. I relate well to people, management, colleagues and customers. I believe I have good sales and marketing techniques when I make any pitch. I have a lot of friends and a happy family life. I believe in living life to the full and I am confident that I am, by balancing my work and leisure environments, generally achieving the goals set out for me in the company's strategic plans.

Friends and family tell me that I should take things slightly easier, but competition is very severe and in order to retain the company's market share, a heavy workload is inevitable.

GROUP VICE-CHAIRMAN (PERSONNEL)'S ASSESSMENT

Most of what the Senior Manager (Sales) says about himself is correct. He is pro-active, does work hard and is good at keeping to a tough schedule. But because he is pushing himself so hard he tends to push others too and it does not always make him as popular as he thinks he is with his staff. He has the reputation for being over-aggressive in his selling techniques and we have evidence that this has actually put some customers off. He is also seriously overweight – due to so much wining and dining of customers, he explains – which means that he goes around in a terrible sweat the whole time, not the best impression to give if a customer is sitting beside him as he explains one of the new software programs to them.

He claims he is balancing his work and leisure time well. This is not quite so, since he admits privately that his wife complains she never sees him, which is probably one of the reasons why his suits (much too small, given his rapidly increasing girth) and his laundry leave much to be desired.

I have tactfully taken him to task on these small points which, added together, currently mar the generally good quality of his work and his sales performance record.

CHAPTER 2

Gut Instincts

Why do some people attract and others
repel … and most get ignored?

A good face is a letter of introduction.
                              Proverb

Appearances are not held to be a clue to the truth. But we seem
to have no other.
                              Ivy Compton-Burnett

Beware that you lose not the substance by grasping at the shadow.
                              Aesop

We automatically lump the people we meet into various categories: those we love, those we like, those we tolerate, those we cannot stand and those – by far the biggest category – whom we totally ignore. We all will have a host of other vaguely defined sub-categories in between. There are certain identifiable positive and negative qualities in inter-personal relationships that cause this to happen. We can learn from this to our advantage.

How do we recognize other people? Among thousands of others at a pop concert we are able to pick out friends from acquaintances or from strangers. How do we do this? Identification relies on us possessing powerful in-built abilities to discriminate between one set of memories of shapes and faces and another. We start, for example, by being able to distinguish most males from most females, even though we don't necessarily comprehend all the factors that constitute masculinity or femininity, and our recognition process is not infallible. As Hobbes said, 'Imagination and Memory are but one thing', and we have all suffered the embarrassment of waving to someone across the street only to realize that we have been greeting a perfect stranger. Recognition of people in stressful situations, for example where a crime has been committed, particularly often leads to cases of mistaken identity. Many theoretical and practical attempts have been made to categorize facial differences, and some studies have attempted to show patterns or physiological landmarks defining the relationship of the eyes, nose and ears to each other, thereby allowing the grouping of various facial types. Such an automatic recognition system is built into every one of us and no matter how unprejudiced we believe we are, we automatically opt in favour of certain facial types and are repelled by others. If you think about it you will certainly recognize this response in yourself.

While to call someone two-faced is a pejorative term, some psychologists argue that each side of the face in fact sends out very different messages. We are all vaguely aware that we have a good side and a bad side (many TV and film stars will only be interviewed if the camera is focused on their favoured profile); because of the way our brain reacts (the left hemisphere controls language while the right reacts and deals with special abilities), we tend to concentrate on the left-hand side of the face when we make judgements about a person. The odd grimace or facial flutter can often reveal deeply hidden meanings. Some people are particularly adept at reading the expressions of others, looking out for the slightest hint or emotional give-away.

Yet a recent Gallup public opinion poll appeared to contradict all this, its results suggesting that most people did not think that they were particularly influenced by the looks or expressions of others. They were specifically asked the following question: 'If you were serving on a jury, to what extent would your verdict be influenced by a defendant's facial looks?' Maybe it was not entirely surprisingly that the vast majority, hoping if not believing that they would always be impartial, said they would not be influenced at all. Sadly, controlled psychological studies show that the reverse is almost universally true and that a significant percentage of any jury or any group of people judging someone coming before them (for example in an interview, which is why the research is so relevant to this book) will be very much swayed by looks. One particularly damning experiment, in which some thousands of people took part, showed that the chances of being found guilty could increase from around 30 per cent to 45 per cent purely on the basis of the defendant's appearance. In simplistic terms this showed that if you 'look like a criminal', you are more likely to be found guilty – the American expression for this being 'negatively defined'. If, on the other hand, you appear handsome and heroic, and don't sweat too much in the witness box, even if you have committed the crime, the chances are that you are more likely to get off. Of course this calls into question what 'looking like a criminal' actually means. But, however defined, there is no doubt that stereo-typed looks always have a big influence on judgements we make of other people. Was it only because Neil Hamilton, the disgraced Tory MP, had a lopsided smile (not that he has had much to smile about recently) that people thought he looked shifty and furtive? Or was it simply that we already had an opinion about him and his 'cash for questions' background, and therefore interpreted his facial char-acteristics as revealing the true character of the man?

The classic case of someone appearing insincere and eventually living up to that reputation, was the disgraced American President Richard Millhouse Nixon. From way back in the early sixties when he appeared on television face to face with the young, charismatic John F. Kennedy, the cameras showed him looking furtive and insecure, eliciting the famous quote: 'Would you buy a used car from this man?' There were always stories that he was undermined by the Kennedy campaign team who manipulated the TV lighting to highlight his famous five o'clock shadow and the sweat on his brow. Pierre Salinger, Kennedy's Press Secretary, later revealed that, by contrast, when the radio audience for these confrontations was polled, it was actually Nixon who won hands down because, without his visual drawbacks, his language was much stronger than Kennedy's hesitant, boyish style of speaking.

There are many ways in which one instinctively believes one knows if one is going to like someone or if they are lying or telling you the truth. Shifty eyes and hesitations may sometimes be enough of a give-away, but a new telephone device, using sophisticated electronics, is now available, which can detect negative tremors in the vocal chords of an untruthful voice. These tremors have to be measured against controlled questions and answers where it is known that the respond-ent is telling the truth. Intended mainly for businessmen who want to know whether someone they are dealing with is honest or not, it is said to be remarkably accurate, particularly in stressed circumstances, for example if a man tells his wife that he is working late and he is in fact dallying elsewhere.

There used to be a toothpaste advertisement, directed at those who were worried about having bad teeth or bad breath, which talked about a 'ring of confidence'. People with that air of trust and confidence about them in other ways, tend to do much better in life than those who appear unsure or insecure. Thus remarks such as 'He appears very suitable', 'She'll do well' and 'John seems like good news' are the common daily terms of approbation for candidates seeking employ-ment or advancement, though, as always, they are mere shorthand comments based on shorthand judgements. In a similar way, Margaret Thatcher would apparently categorize people as being, or not being, 'one of us', tending to cast into political oblivion those who were not. Just as everyone finds beauty in a different kind of face, so do we all, despite our best intentions, rush to make instant judgements about others the moment we set eyes on them. Life is too short to delay making such an appraisal.

On the basis of previous experience, we like to think that we know instinctively what someone else is or will be like. 'I go on gut instinct and I'm usually right,' we say to ourselves, since that has generally been our experience in the past. If we like someone very much, as with a sweetheart, we focus on all their positive qualities and down-grade any annoying little habits they may have, though these, as we all know, may play a negative part in later life. In less extreme cases, the same principles apply. Yet, recognizing all this, when it comes to us presenting ourselves to other people, we still make few serious, conscious attempts to take advantage of this knowledge and sit down and work out how to present our own positive attributes in a rational and attractive way. Even if we have had some of our weaknesses clearly pointed out to us in annual appraisal interviews or management reviews, we often do little to rectify matters and try to marginalize them, usually concentrating on moaning about the person or the system that has had the impertinence to criticize us.

Liking and Disliking

As we have seen, some people attract and others repel us not just as a result of some in-built prejudice, but because we are too busy to suspend judgement for long – about strangers, about colleagues, about politicians, about anyone. We 'read' only the most obvious signals, then automatically brand them as kind, stupid, pretty, boring, ugly, bad-tempered. To prove it, try this simple game. When you next watch television, mark public figures and other performers, including the newsreaders, from 1 to 10 in terms of their dress sense, their posture and appearance, the sound and texture of their voice, and whether you would buy a used car from them, let alone vote for them. This begins to expand on what the Primacy Effect is really about and how you can learn to develop yours.

From time to time we come across people who are a real turn-off. This can be because of the personality that they project, something to do with their physical appearance, or it can be because of the causes they espouse. Research shows that when Gerry Adams or Ian Paisley appears on television, a huge majority of mainland British audiences

We all have preconceptions: Is this figure commanding or inflammatory?

tend neither to listen nor believe anything they say. A reputation for dubious dealing leads us to look for dubious characteristics, such as some see in Mohamed Al Fayed, the proprietor of the London store, Harrods, who has spent so much of his money in ensuring that the causes in which he has had an interest have been well ventilated by those British MPs who accepted brown envelopes from him. Another politician who is widely seen as failing in sincerity terms is New York Senator Alfonse D'Amato. Descriptive adjectives about him change only slightly depending on the commentator, but words such as 'irritating' and 'smarmy' appear in almost everything written about him.

As well as having what the pollsters call 'name recognition', his widely mocked New York Italian accent also grants him 'voice recognition', as befits a politician who believes that the first duty of a politician is to get re-elected, and to ensure that he does whatever wins favour with New York's voters.

Name recognition is a fascinating subject. One of the names that in the industrial and financial world is bandied about probably more than anyone else's is that of Allan Greenspan, the Chairman of the US Federal Reserve Bank. He is a man who, when he lets go an unguarded word, which he seldom does, causes the world's economy to shake. Everyone knows his name, everyone knows the effect he has on the economies of nations. Very few people know him or would recognize him. By contrast, mention the name Jean Chretien and most in the world would say 'Who?' He is currently the Prime Minister of Canada, a nation strong, powerful and prosperous, yet whose leaders are largely unknown outside its borders. Who remembers any Canadian leader since Pierre Trudeau? Even he was known largely because of the beauty and errant behaviour of his wife.

Physical turn-offs are not just to do with looks but with skin texture, whether someone sweats a lot, whether they've shaved or have the two days' growth which is currently fashionable in certain areas of life but is a certain negative in more mature company. Restless eyes or a permanently aggressive look will, equally, force people to look away or avoid the person concerned.

Many specific academic studies over the years have tried to determine why people like or dislike their fellow men and women. One of the most common experiments is a test called the 'Family Systems Exercise', where strangers are put together in a room and asked to select those who make them feel most at home. A huge majority pick partners who are later revealed to have very similar emotional and educational histories and backgrounds, but there are a number of other reasons for 'liking' as well, largely to do with behaviour as well as appearance, dress style and voice tones.

The Recency Effect

While the Primacy Effect has us typecasting or typecasted from the first moment because it saves time and it is very convenient to us to categorize individuals in as consistent a way as possible, later experience of them can bring enchantment or disenchantment in its wake. 'I realize he's not my type' or 'I don't like her sort' may be a prejudiced and wrong way of going through life but we are all to some extent guilty of the practice. After a first meeting, our attitude towards that person will change only very slowly, but if our meetings with them subsequently become frequent, or if there is a long gap between encounters, then, for better or worse, our *most proximate* experience of them, what psychologists call the *Recency Effect*, takes over in importance.

Not only do the Primacy and Recency Effects apply to our attitudes to individuals (as they do, incidentally, to inanimate things and situations – we say, 'That picture is growing on me', or 'I'm getting used to working here'), most importantly they also apply to the message a person may be delivering. 'I don't like his face so I'm not going to listen to him' may appear brutal, but it's probably been your subconscious judgement of someone or other in course of the last 24 hours. Irrespective of the individual and his qualities, we usually know precisely how we are going to react to someone trying to sell us Bible tracts at our front door or a beggar attempting to waylay us in the street. We believe we know from experience what their plea is going to be, and we are probably going to dismiss it before it is even uttered.

Gut Reactions

The most cautious and the least judgemental of us are no different from the rest when it comes to how speedily, and often inaccurately, we assess our fellow men and women in this way. Even the most painstaking of us are overwhelmingly persuaded by those gut reactions which seldom permit us to give the people we encounter a second chance. When we see someone for the first time, that initial Sound/Vision Bite – a combination of their looks, their dress, their bearing, and the tenor of their opening remarks, if they even get that far – becomes deeply etched in our minds and affects our future attitudes to them. Ill-delivered and badly chosen words or an unpleasant voice that jars on our ears, an inappropriate gesture or an unfortunate dress code, can do a huge amount of instant damage. Style buries substance. If someone goes in for nose-rings or nose-picking, or they have dirty fingernails, not matter how effective they are reputed to be at their jobs, they are quite simply not going to fit your bill. Whatever your attitude is to people who smoke, for example, there is a great deal of evidence that, in this politically correct age, smokers lose out on a great number of jobs because of their habit. Pre-set assumptions you have about others and their character traits are known by psychologists as *implicit personal theories*. Without a lot of hard work, overcoming these initial prejudices or prejudgements is a long process, particularly because anything that person does in subsequent sightings has a tendency merely to reinforce your view that your first basic reaction was the correct one. Clothes that need dry cleaning or unwashed hair will tend to mark out someone who you instinctively believe will be sloppy and uncaring in their professional life and work as well. If you in turn have nasty little habits (some of which you may not recognize or know about because no one has had the courage to tell you) you will suffer this same treatment. We are all instantly predefined in other people's minds, not just by our backgrounds, or upbringing, our professions and our looks, but by every single item of our behaviour, even the way we eat, which brands us before we get to say a word.

Judging by Appearances

Having the right build and physical presence for the job you are seeking to fill is surprisingly important as well. You look for a builder who is strong; you expect your great opera singers to be vast, though not necessarily quite as vast as Pavarotti. Good lawyers should be sparsely built, just as chefs should be round and jovial, though they seldom are. Equally, you expect your princesses to be slim and beautiful like the late Princess of Wales rather than the figure of fun which the Duchess of York has latterly become. The overall build and appearance of those who lecture you – priests, politicians or telepundits, for example – should command a special respect. Back in the late 1980s, how much more valid and believable Margaret Thatcher's then overweight Chancellor, Nigel Lawson, would have been when he talked about the nation's need of belt-tightening and so on, had he looked as trim as he does today.

If there is one person on the international stage whose appearance counts heavily against him in the eyes of most people in the Western world it is Yassir Arafat. Long after his terrorist background has been forgotten outside Israel, the fact that he appears as an ugly, badly shaved, scruffy individual, always glistening with sweat in front of the cameras, hardly makes him a favourable symbol for the aspirations of the Palestinian people. By contrast, Nelson Mandela, with his charm, his smile and his sparkling eyes, even though, through age, the latter are growing somewhat faded, has made him an icon of the age, someone who is found to be thoroughly wholesome, gentle, forgiving and wise. His reputation is, very decidedly, not shared by his former wife Winnie who, despite her strong following and sparky presence, has largely written herself out of South African politics.

False images abound. Pol Pot ranks alongside Hitler and Stalin as one of the most evil despots of all time. Yet when he finally appeared on our television screens at his trial, having been captured after being betrayed by his followers, he looked merely like a tired old man.

Behaviour, etiquette (which is codified manners) and general demeanour are other especially strong factors in why you take against or for someone, since you are conditioned to believe that they indicate how he or she will function in other areas of activity. If someone does not stand up when a senior or older person comes into a room, it may not just be read as a mark of indolence or rudeness, but of an attitude to life, which those involved may not wish to have to put up with in their working environment. Interestingly enough, there have been many controlled surveys which show that well-behaved and well-turned-out people are believed to be more interesting, wealthier and more likely to make better marriage partners. While matrimonial choice patterns are beyond the scope of this book, and while there is little scientific evidence for this, that is what people believe. By contrast, a skinhead wearing a Union Jack T-shirt and waving a half-full can of lager at us may be attractive to some, but will send most of the rest of us much more negative messages because of stereotyping and the knowledge we have of past events involving people like him. Gestalt psychologists – that is those who believe that individuals are perceived as whole entities rather than having complex strands in their make-up – are not alone in arguing that we lump people into categories by age, by social background and occupation, by sex and by overall appearance, and that then, and only then, we very reluctantly distinguish them by subgrouping. That the person we perceived as a mere lager-lout is a church-going computer whizz-kid who loves his mother, is a fact that tends to get lost without a lot of help from other evidence. Prejudice is the culprit: physical image brings a whole range of positive or negative baggage along with it which is unsubstantiated by what is actually there. People have to look the part.

At the other end of the spectrum from the lager-lout, take the case of Sir Richard Greenbury, who was used to living a relatively unpublic life as the distinguished Chairman of Marks and Spencer, one of Britain's most successful companies. He made what in due course he doubtless felt was the mistake of hitting the headlines as Chairman of the Committee of Inquiry looking into what the general public felt were hugely inflated Directors' Remunerations. Those who watched the dismissive yet lacklustre way in which he presented his report, or who saw his furious reaction to the subsequent pillorying he received from the media, would not, I believe, have given Sir Richard high marks on a charisma scale of one to ten. Did that matter? Yes. Why? Because there was an important case to be made in the report itself, and it was not well done. Sir Richard's image, like the lager-lout's, conditioned his audience's reaction, and the report's findings got stifled by the mere telling of it.

Image, message and character are totally intertwined. One famous piece of research involved presenting groups of people with a list of adjectives describing a fictitious person. One group was given the following characteristics to define that person: intelligent, skilful, industrious, warm, determined, practical and cautious. A second group was given exactly the same list, except that the word 'cold' took the place of the word 'warm'. These lists were called Stimulus Lists. Both groups each were then presented with a second list of eighteen trait words, all different from the so-called Stimulus List and they were then asked to underline those which described the so-called Target or fictional person. The two groups chose significantly different words from the second list. The 'warm' group saw the character as being generous, humorous, sociable and popular, while the 'cold' group saw the fictional person as having largely negative traits. Certain other qualities were attributed to the fictional person by both groups, for example reliable, persistent, restrained, strong and honest, but from this particular experiment the simple words 'warm' and 'cold' triggered off strong impressions, without any other justification, that one person was friendly and popular while the other was unfriendly and unpopular.

What has all this got to do with you and your individual Primacy Effect? As numerous other studies have shown, the Halo or so-called Global Perception Effect is one to which everyone you come across will adhere, to one degree or another. It all boils down to the fact that we all like to see people in as consistent a way as possible, and find it simpler to regard someone as having either all good qualities or all bad qualities rather than a mixture of both. You don't need psychologists to tell you that the most extreme form of this Halo Effect is when you are in love, and you see your partner as totally faultless. By contrast, any enemies you may have bring upon themselves a whole range of vile and vicious adjectives with considerable ease. If someone burgles your house and then ends up in court, you will be extremely generous if you recognize many redeeming qualities in the person who has wronged you.

While the fundamental principle of the Primacy Effect is that the first thing you experience is the most long-lasting, there is a lot of evidence to suggest that later information about someone which seems to disprove your initial reaction to them, will actually be discounted by your saying to yourself that the 'real person' was the one you first met or identified. Secondary material is dismissed as not being representative or typical of that individual. This adds weight to the argument that the Primacy Effect is more powerful than the Recency Effect in most situations, not least because we simply ignore any later, conflicting information that comes our way. Obviously if there has been a very long gap between your first encounter with somebody and your second, then the Recency Effect in reality becomes a second shot at the Primacy Effect. Equally it goes without saying that, as you get to know people as friends or close colleagues and you see a great deal of them, then the Recency Effect takes over completely. You gradually pick up their myriad faults and attributes that have lain hidden. But as far as the subject of this book is concerned – the impression you make on strangers or people who do not know you particularly well, when parading yourself at an interview, arguing a case, or selling some product – the overriding potency of the Primacy Effect remains paramount.

Behaviour Patterns

Irrespective of who is the current occupant of a particular job in any organization, there are certain levels of behaviour and deportment that you expect from them. You have pre-set assumptions about what they should think and feel and even what they should look like. You cannot have an Archbishop of Canterbury, a Major General or the Chairman of a bank looking or acting as if they had been selected from some collective of down-and-outs. You do not expect your Chief Executive to get drunk and disorderly in public any more than you would expect your MP to be found cavorting in some dubious night-club. If you yourself behave 'properly' and in keeping with your status, the smoother your relationships will be. Knowing what is expected of you and matching your role models thus become other critical factors in any assessment process. It is not just an individual who has to watch his or her reputation. The same goes for those associated with them. Whatever one thinks of his politics, Benjamin Netanyahu, the Prime Minister of Israel, is at first glance a good-looking man with an attractive voice, but he has suffered badly as a result of his wife's reputation as an extremely difficult woman who sacks nannies and blows her top over some of his political associates. World history is peppered with people who have benefited or suffered from the repu-tation of their wives. Would we still remember, for example, President Peron of Argentina, were it not for the worldwide reputation of his wife Eva? Would President Reagan have stood taller or smaller without the drive and resourceful if shrewish behaviour of his wife Nancy?

Most of us in our professional lives expect certain other norms of behaviour. Unless you are a policeman or a social worker, you do not expect people you meet to hit you or swear at you or otherwise behave disgracefully. Some areas of activity, however, seem to be particularly cursed with people who behave badly. In European football, Paul Gascoigne is one *enfant terrible*, while Mike Tyson is the beast of the boxing ring, and the atrocious behaviour of the Gallagher brothers has made the name Oasis mean what it does to the pop world. But equally in business and political life there are many people whose behaviour has been criticized for one reason or another. Daily, the pages of the *Financial Times* are filled with tales of the crimes or shady dealings of people like Asil Nadir, sullying the good name of commerce or the City.

Many people put us off not because of their bad behaviour so much as that they appear snobbish and pompous in everything that they say. The upper class bray of the chairman of a local golf club, because of the little brief authority he appears to have inherited, drives the rest of us up the wall. No doubt Jonathan Aitken, the talented but flawed and disgraced former MP, would have had a far better press had he not been so sneering and superior every time he came face to face with his fellow men and women in the past. As an aside, a fascinating if politically incorrect behavioural study of ethnic groups in the United States (Italian, German, Jewish etc) asked a polled group to describe each nationality according to a series of 84 different adjectives. The results showed a disturbing amount of agreement, particularly with reference to derogatory terms and traits, thus giving further evidence of the dangerous bias but the incontrovertible reality of stereotyping.

Personal Identity

Looking at how you yourself appear, the Fifteen-Second Rule is near absolute. Your appearance, facial expressions and general demeanour have to match the occasion. If you dress badly, if you speak with a lack of clarity or assurance, if you look nervous or bored, unless your reputation has in some way already been very fully and firmly established, as we will explore in later chapters, you will be prejudged by these characteristics which will be seen as your personal, defining signature. Just as a company has a logo, that catalogue of attributes will be yours – your *Personal Identity*. Fifteen seconds to reach a judgement is not long, but in practice most people and audiences don't have an attention span that is much longer than that. That, as advertisers have always recognized, is why you have to move quickly and say a lot in the shortest possible time. You have to have the first word. You have to grab people's attention from the outset. You normally only have one chance. A cruel fact, but true.

Image is just as important in corporate life. I can remember being amused when I first went to the United States many years ago and encountered my first hot-air hand-drier in a Boston comfort station. It had a delightful graffito scrawled across it: 'Press here for a message from your Senator'. Image creation is not just hot air: sometimes it works and sometimes it does not. Some PR campaigns have proved very effective in defining a company's standing in the public mind; others have had the reverse effect. There are signs everywhere that the hot air generated by advertising and PR campaigns waged by big public corporations, for example, particularly the privatized utilities telling everybody how much they care about everything, is beginning to grate on the public consciousness. We do not want some gas company chairman or the managing director of a privatized water company talking about caring. What we want is good, cheap gas and plentiful supplies of water from companies that do not appear to be ripping off the public through spending too much money on senior executive perks or excessive payouts to shareholders. The trouble often lies in the fact that, no matter how good the spokespersons are, the fundamental truth about the Primacy Effect is again pre-eminent: once a corporate image has stuck, it is very difficult to dislodge.

Prejudice

Psychologists have irrefutable proof that, fight it as you may, you are going to be prejudiced for or against certain types of people. No one is immune to prejudice. Even if it is not over such blatant matters as race or social class, it will be there, whether it has to do with age or sex considerations, what part of the country someone comes from, how personable they look, how clearly they speak and with what accent, or how they stand, sit, eat or dress. No matter what the content, you will be much more likely to be convinced if a message or presentation is delivered with sufficient confidence and authority by someone whom you relate well to, someone who is like you, someone from a familiar peer group, someone who stands tall and inspires your immediate respect and confidence. The panoply of high office, for example a message coming to you from the MD or CEO, will make you listen especially intently, if only out of awe. By contrast, someone lower down the tree or 'alien' who converses in grunts and looks as if he has been sleeping in his clothes, will fail in all attempts to get his message through to you. Just occasionally the opposite is true. Would we know very much about Peru's President Alberto Fujimori, were he not of Japanese origin? It is this that makes him stand apart from all the other leaders in South America. By contrast, Australia has long been known for people who are larger than life and who have cut a swathe through normal roles in accepted business life, sometimes successfully like Rupert Murdoch, and sometimes unsuccessfully like the great yachting hero, Alan Bond, whose business empire collapsed so catastrophically.

When they are going to have to present themselves or a case to someone, so many people forget that their overall presence and the way they say things, the whole tenor and authority of their voices, are much more important than agonizing over the precise words that they intend using. They spend days deciding what they are going to say at a presentation or in an interview. They spend little or no time on working out *how* they will say it, not realizing that communicating, even at that level, is like acting. Actors and actresses train for years to put resonance and credibility into the parts they play, since, unless they are believable, the critics will hammer them. As in a theatre, any audience, from a single interviewer sitting at the other side of an office table to a thousand people in a great conference hall, has to be inspired to listen to you, and not by your words alone. The overall personal impact you make is crucial.

If you think hard about people you know and respect, you will realize you have gradually grown to value them because of their judgement, their intelligence, their general all-round wisdom, their personality, their charm, their leadership qualities, their technical skills and so on. In an interview, however, no one is given much of a chance to display these qualities. Nevertheless, as you will see in later chapters, you can, with careful planning, make a good stab at getting certain key messages through. Given that in most job recruitment interviews and headhunting exercises, your professional qualifications and other background information about you, your work experience and the testimonials of your former employers, are all taken as given, it is the bit beyond that makes the difference as to whether you even get to the first interview. No matter how balanced a scrutineer is, there is evidence that less experienced interviewers tend to select like-minded neo-clones of themselves. Though professionals will make every effort to stay clear of any such bias, if there are plenty of candidates to choose from, he or she will go for people whom they find appealing under the categories listed above. Occasionally something equally well-defined if not as common, called the attraction of opposites, does emerge, though it is a particularly difficult hypothesis to test. In interviews between people of opposite sexes, gender aspects also come into play, a subject that will be touched upon later. Suffice it to say here that there are huge positive and negative attitudes built into any cross-gender interview.

These then are some of the reasons why we react in such remarkably different ways when new people swim into our ken. One man's meat is another's poison in human relationships as well. Some people are naturally gregarious and popular, others shy and introverted. While it may appear that the former group is going to stand a much better chance in life, there are very many employment opportunities where the latter category would be more welcome. Whatever type you are, you can succeed equally well, provided you make yourself fully aware of your underlying strengths and how you should play them to best advantage.

'What are you going to do about her?' asked Dr Mackenzie. She and Bill had just passed through the reception area and were returning to his office.

'You talking about the receptionist?' asked Bill.

'The same,' said Ruth Mackenzie.

'Joanna's quite sweet. She's reasonably good at taking messages.' Bill shrugged.

'She's the first impression you give visitors as to what this company is all about.'

'OK. She doesn't dress very well and her hair is a mess. But what does it really matter . . .' Bill had other work to get on with. Ruth was on a timewaster.

'My point exactly,' said Ruth. 'She's always smoking behind the reception desk or painting her nails and waiting for them to dry. Meanwhile guests queue up until she feels like answering their questions. Phones ring too long unanswered, and that whole reception area is in a mess. All those dead plants. Isn't that her job too?'

'Yes, I suppose . . .' said Bill, reluctantly. 'But she is rather sweet. Everybody quite likes her.'

'Rather . . . quite . . . Don't you think it would be better for her future career too if someone pointed some of her defects out to her?' said Ruth Mackenzie. 'I'm not suggesting you sack her, but having her as the up-front welcome sign to this business, she's a No No. Remember what I said about the Fifteen-Second Rule? It works for that whole reception area as well, I can tell you. And while we are on the question of impressions, d'you mind if I mention something personal once again, Bill?' she went on.

'Fire away.' Bill sighed and glanced at his watch. 'I have yet to meet the woman who could shake my confidence in myself.'

'Is that a challenge? OK, here goes,' said Dr Mackenzie. 'Apart from your shirt collar curl problem ... I'm back to the vexed question of your tie.'

'A girlfriend gave it to me.'

'You told me that. Obviously a treasured relic.'

'The girlfriend?' Bill smiled briefly. 'I've had it cleaned.'

'I noticed, but the bin might have been a better place. Don't you realize, Bill, that a tie is the focal point of a man's dress? Deliberately so. That is where everybody focuses, at least most of the time.'

'Come off it. You're on to the colour-me-pretty school. Do you want us all dressed in Armani suits?' Bill was indignant. It was getting beyond a joke.

'Certainly not. But ...' Ruth Mackenzie paused then gently began to flatter. 'You've got a great future ahead of you, Bill. JD thinks very highly of you. The time has come for you to look and dress the part. You've got so much going for you, it would be a pity to spoil it at the edges.'

Bill looked embarrassed for a moment, then looked up at her. 'OK,' he said, with a mischievous gleam. 'Work me over.'

PERSONAL ASSESSMENT REPORT: CASE STUDY NO. 1

PERSONAL AND CONFIDENTIAL, FOR CANDIDATE X

ASSESSMENT BY CASE PARTNER, A & B EXECUTIVE SEARCH

Following your lack of success in being selected for the position of Managing Director, you asked me for a strictly personal assessment as to why, when you did so well at the preliminary interviews and easily got on to our shortlist, you fell at the final hurdle. You asked me to be extremely frank. This I am going to be since I believe you have outstanding professional and managerial qualities and would have filled the job with great skill and determination.

First of all, there is no question that your background skills and the senior positions you have held in the past fully justified your being put on our shortlist. But I warned you from the outset that, while I and my colleagues at A & B Executive Search have got to know and recognize these abilities and aptitudes, you did not necessarily demonstrate them on first meeting. As you yourself recognize, you are admirably modest about your many achievements. You feel that it is for others to sing your praises; indeed the letters of recommendation you have had from all your referees were warm if not glowing.

To be quite blunt, you let yourself down badly when you appeared for your final interview with the Chairman of the Board. From what we had said about you, he had expected you to shine, but despite our having strongly recommended that you fully rehearsed what you wanted to say, you came across, according to our sources, as somewhat lacklustre, even disinterested in the senior position you were seeking to fill.

Perhaps you worried too much about the interview in advance. Maybe you had not slept particularly well – only you will know the answer to that. But from the moment you came into the boardroom, you seemed ill at ease and lacked the alertness that I know you can clearly demonstrate. That in the end let you down.

I know from our discussions in the past that you yourself, when you are recruiting people to work for you, are always very chary about going by appearances. You think that many selection processes are highly superficial in this regard. You are right on both counts, but that, sadly, is the way of the world.

RECOMMENDATION

I strongly recommend that before we put your name forward again for another senior appointment in keeping with your experience, you undertake a brief course on interview and self-presentation skills. You will need such abilities more and more in the future. I say this in all honesty, since I and my colleagues believe you have great aptitudes and a capacity to improve markedly as you move to fill greater and ever more high-profile positions in your industry in the years ahead.

Once you have identified who is going to give you this training, I would be happy to brief him or her on where I and my colleagues feel improvement is most needed.

CHAPTER 3

How We Communicate

Words, non-verbal communication,
paralanguage, body language and all that

When the eyes say one thing and the tongue another,
a practised man relies on the language of the first.
Ralph Waldo Emerson

It is only the shallow people who do not judge by appearances.
Oscar Wilde

First know who you are, then adorn yourself accordingly.
Epictetus

Costly thy habit as thy purse can buy,
But not express'd in fancy; rich, not gaudy;
For the apparel oft proclaims the man.
Shakespeare, Hamlet

I'd still be President if I had communicated better.
George Bush

W hen we communicate with each other we are constantly looking for and sending a whole host of non-verbal signs and signals. We emit and receive messages in ways that are much more complex and telling than if conveyed by words alone. We note how close someone stands, their posture, their gestures, their other body language and above all, their facial expressions. All these things, plus the crucial factor of their paralanguage – voice tone, pauses, cadences, rhythm and so on – condition what we hear and how much we understand.

We know what we want to say. We think we are saying it. But is there anyone out there listening? And even if we think and they think they are hearing us, are we confident that they *understand* what we are trying to say? Then again, if they do hear and understand, do they believe us, or does our whole facial and body language and our paralanguage give us away?

Researchers at the University of East Anglia have developed a computer that can lip-read without the need for a traditional keyboard. The system identifies the letters and words being spoken by recognizing the measurements of mouth movements, thus complementing the speech recognition computers that are already widely available in the marketplace, but which only work properly in otherwise sound-free environments. Just as we try to understand what people are saying to us in a noisy bar, these computers, like humans, read the facial language as we do, and understand the responses even if no words are heard. In such circumstances we see that visual clues become much more important than the words. The words 'Yes I would like another drink' may be inaudible above the noise and laughter in a pub, for example, but a smile, a nod and a thumbs-up will be fully understood.

We are all adept, to a greater or lesser extent, at lip-reading, for example with someone we know when we do not want to be overheard. The deaf are forced to develop extra skills in this direction. If we have to lip-read, for secrecy reasons, because we are curious about someone else's whispered conversation, or because we cannot hear the other person as a result of background noise, we often do it quite effectively. The tabloid newspapers have in the past employed expert lip-readers, who study film taken by video cameras, to discover what the rich and famous are saying to one another at a great distance, and the CIA are said to have developed this expertise to a high degree of accuracy, assisted by what they pick up from powerful directional microphones.

Standing on their own, without any paralanguage, words can matter to us if they are of sufficient informational importance. Bernard Shaw once said that if the Archbishop of Canterbury says 'God exists', it is all in a day's work. If he ever says 'God does not exist', then 'something significant has been said'. We would all sit up at that statement, no matter how flatly delivered. A railway company announcement that a train has been delayed, or the voice that is the speaking clock, does not need any feeling injected into it to ensure that its message is received and understood.

Having considered the in-built, automatic process of making a judgement about someone when we first meet them, we moved on to examine how we guess at their likely attitudes and reactions to other individuals, situations, and events, from the visual clues they give us. As a third step we now need to look at the deliberate measures we all take to communicate our emotions and ideas without necessarily having recourse to words. The psychological term for this process is *non-verbal leakage*. We see when people are obviously happy, sad, resigned, defiant, confident or insecure. Unless they deliberately hide their emotions, we often read from their facial expressions and body language, long before they begin speaking, whether they are likely to be respectful or insolent, nervous or at their ease, even whether they are in a mood to agree or disagree with us.

We read what we think we see. We use a vast number of tiny muscles to change our facial expressions, and these gradually become etched in if we use them constantly. The types of lines on any face end up giving away far more than advancing age. The actual shape of a face will also be read: a round soft face suggests a similar personality; a square and rugged jawline gives the impression of tough determination. A lopsided smile may be quaint and charming to some and shifty to others.

As anyone in the hospitality industry knows, the first impression that a guest has when they first enter a hotel or restaurant sets the tone for their entire stay. That is why people on tourism training courses are taught that a first genuine smile, giving the impression of a guest being really welcome, is critical. We all know the effect on us if an office receptionist is surly, or if we are given scant attention in a shop or bar. No matter how good the food or product, if the service is offhand then the whole occasion is spoiled or the sale is lost. We marvel at how airline stewards and stewardesses manage to parade a welcoming 'Good evening, Sir' and 'Welcome aboard, Ma'am' to a hundred passengers several times in the course of any working day when they can hardly mean it. Yet it is merely an extreme form of the act that all of us put on all the time.

While a warm greeting from a waiter or airline stewardess may add something to our meal or flight, a brittle empty smile can be as telling as the cold stare and the steely blue eyes that sometimes open up a tense business meeting. Like the act of shaking hands which was originally intended to show the person you were greeting that you were not carrying a dagger (though we all recognize that only one hand is used for shaking and the other one can still conceal any amount of threat), the smile of meeting and greeting establishes an instant rapport.

With experience we improve our ability to read non-facial as well as facial signs – for example, noting nervous tics or hands that constantly play with spectacles or with hair. Television cameramen sometimes play tricks by cutting from a politician's cool controlled face to where the hands or feet are trembling. Long ago Sigmund Freud recorded this observation: 'He that has eyes to see and ears to hear will realize that no one can keep a secret. If his lips are silent, he *chatters with his fingertips*. Betrayal oozes out of every pore.'

Body Language and All That

From visible signs, for example, you get the 'feeling' when someone is not being strictly honest with you: a nervous grin, a trembling knee, a tendency to sweat, or a forced smile that is not carried through to the eyes. Whatever the words spoken, if the accompanying body language fails to convince, then the message is inadequately conveyed. Psychological research has proved conclusively that in interpersonal communication, the visual impression you make – that is your *presence*, along with the sound, tone and authority of your voice, what is known as your *paralanguage* – has a vastly greater effect on others than the actual words you use. In some studies, social scientists have discovered that words amount to less than ten per cent of the overall message: saying 'yes', for example, when the entire body and paralanguage is shouting out 'no', is a false message that can be all too clearly read by others. General posture can very clearly be 'read'. If you stand at a slouch with hunched shoulders, you will look forlorn and dejected, even if your lips say 'I'm OK', whereas if you stand tall with your shoulders back and your hands on your hips you look confident and defiant.

Some psychologists also read a great deal into the way people sit when listening to one another. Sit upright, lean towards you interlocutor and you are in responsive mood. Sit back or look away and the reverse is true, even though your head may be nodding in apparent agreement. But the most important channel of non-verbal communication of all is the eyes; prolonged eye-contact is not only a sign of attraction and attention but can, in varying degrees, mark out a whole range of emotions and inter-relationships. By contrast, passing acquaintances will glance at each other only momentarily, unwilling to adopt lingering stares that might be perfectly suitable to mutually attractive members of the opposite sex.

A huge amount has been written about a look in the eyes that characterizes successful men and women. I can remember one of Tiny Rowland's adversaries saying he felt almost mesmerized every time he caught the gaze of that secretive businessman. Equally, Tony Blair's eyes, as the much-derided 'demon-eyes' poster used in the Tory election campaign demonstrated, do indeed mark out that particular politician. The fervour of his message is emphasized by the ardour of his looks. And we all remember that famous remark made by President Mitterand about Margaret Thatcher – that she had 'the lips of Marilyn Monroe and the eyes of Caligula'.

Many people go through life thinking they are communicating well but doing so badly. As a result they suffer both socially and in their working careers. With business colleagues, in particular, they adopt a take-it-or-leave-it attitude. 'I am what I am,' they say. They don't try, arguing that those who do, who have the gift of the gab or are too pushy and full of themselves, get ridiculed and fall by the wayside of life. All too many make very little effort to see themselves as others do. Yet the higher up the business or social ladder they get, the more important their overall 'presence' or public image, their ability to speak in public or be interviewed credibly and well, becomes. The man or woman who would be Chief Executive or Sales Director has to look and sound a good performer on the platforms of business and professional life.

Reinforcing the message

As we have seen, we all communicate with each other, and with a wider world, in a huge variety of ways – with a smile, a nod, a clenched fist, a shrug or a wink. When we talk, we stress some words, raise the pitch of our voice at the end of a question, or pause dramatically to draw attention to a particular point. Most of us use a whole range of verbal and non-verbal exclamation marks all the time. Those who do not, who speak in a flat, quiet, unaccentuated monotone, are on permanent switch-off mode with their colleagues. Our personal range of non-verbal communication devices help us make our point.

Some psychologists and sociologists believe that human beings are thus 'acting' much of the time, putting on a series of performances to suit the situations with which they are faced. We all do this, for example with children, where we will fake anger, pleasure or amusement to warn or entertain them. The premier actor/politician of the post-war period was of course President Ronald Reagan who, above all, read his lines extremely well. In California I once watched him in close-up being briefed by his aides, who told him what his thinking on Nicaragua was on that day, what he should say about the Middle East if questioned, and then saw him handed a speech which he had not seen but which, with broken-up words and lots of hints in the text, they assured him he would deliver to perfection, even without rehearsal. This approach by his presidential puppet-masters was exemplified by the famous quote by his speech-writer Peggy Noonan, who later wrote: 'The battle for the mind of Ronald Reagan was like trench warfare in World War I; never had so many battled so hard over such barren terrain.' Politics in the United States, as elsewhere in the world, is riddled with personalities who have acted out parts for better or for worse. Newt Gingrich, for example, when he emerged from the lower echelons of politics, for a brief time became the superhuman face of the future of American politics. Then, as House Speaker, he began to slip, and, as always, it was as he fell that the media started putting the boot in.

If we take this theory that life is all an act to its extreme, then the real self is invisible – all we are showing in any given set of circumstances is a mask or façade to match the moment and to influence how others perceive us, something that is known as *impression management*. Absurd as that may sound – and few dispute that we all have inherent qualities and characteristics which are constantly on parade – we are forced to put on an act for some of the time. The announcement that someone has died, for instance, may not affect us at all on an emotional level, but we will still put on a grave face suitable to the occasion, thus, if not artificially matching the grief of those around us, at least not greeting the news with an inane grin on our face. Equally, we spend a lot of time *not* letting our emotions show, either because it would be bad form, or because we don't want to show our hand, for example in the middle of a tough business negotiation, or for other reasons to make us socially acceptable.

The 50/40/10 Breakdown

The visual impact of the human communication process is greatly underestimated and frequent studies, not only by psychologists but also by business and time-and-motion consultants, have demonstrated conclusively that, in many communications between two private individuals or between a speaker and his or her audience, well over 50 per cent of the message is delivered by *the image and body language of the speaker*, around 40 per cent by the character, timbre and strength of the voice, that is, *the elements of sound other than the words*, or in other words their *paralanguage*, and, amazingly, only 10 per cent or less by the words themselves. (Again I am not talking about the sort of purely factual communication such as that given at any airport about flight times or other precise exchanges of information.) Other well-researched studies argue that even in two-person conversations, the verbal component of the meaning is often only 35 per cent against 65 per cent for the non-verbal. This merely underlines the old saying about a look conveying more than a thousand words. After all, especially when we know people very well, we frequently 'converse' without opening our mouths at all. Looks can kill. Any husband and wife, father and child, or angry employer and his or her employee, would wholeheartedly agree. Sometimes all this is bundled up into general terms such as of body language, creating a rapport, or building up an emotional or interpersonal appeal. There is a lot more to it than just that.

Paralanguage

We live in a media-dominated society where, as we move to the top of our chosen career, our public reputation begins to matter as much as, if not more than, how good we are in private. A few ill-chosen or ill-delivered words, a lack of tact in dealing with our employees, and how we express ourselves in front of others, can do great and lasting damage. So why do many otherwise successful people make so little effort to improve? One reason for this fault or default, particularly in Anglo-Saxon societies, is the in-built distrust that exists of those who are too quick with words, too outspoken, too verbally gushing, too glib, too clever by half. We are wary of what Americans call 'empty suits' – the smile-nice, talk-nice, soft-soap people. We tend to think that our background qualities should somehow emerge into the foreground of their own accord and speak for themselves. By contrast, what is dramatic in one part of the world seems tedious in another. The 'speaking clock'- type recriminations and apologies which have, over the years, come from successive Japanese Prime Ministers and government officials, and from their counterparts in South Korea, deploring and apologizing for various bribery and other political scandals, have less effect on the rest of the world by the very nature of their perceived delivery. The unaccented way in which the language comes across the airwaves, the lack of discernible paralanguage, means that, despite the underlying drama, the news story fails to grip.

We expect people who address us regularly on radio and television to have a particular clarity of speech, even though there are one or two eccentric exceptions who successfully break the rule. A prime example is the weather forecaster Ian McCaskill, who has built up something of a reputation for himself by the very nature of his convoluted vowel

Have you got a grip on your audience?

sounds as he reads the forecast. He has risen above the defect of not having perfect diction because a degree of pleasant eccentricity, in British society, outweighs normal conversational conventions. As an aside here, our attitude to black and oriental races if we are white, or vice versa, is always a dangerous subject on which to comment. Here again, we all have our stereotypes, though some people manage to rise above them. Trevor Macdonald, for example, the West-Indian-born television newsreader, is not only a pre-eminent exponent of the Queen's English, but also Chairman of a committee set up to try to improve the standards of speech among Britain's schoolchildren.

Most of the rest of us communicate reasonably well in day-to-day conversation. We get by. But there are crucial skills we need to develop if we want to increase our prospects and standing with a wider, or a more selective and demanding audience. As children, we mostly learnt to speak and be understood around the age of two or three, long before we were able to read and write. Seldom do the majority of us get or seek any further instruction in later life on how to enunciate clearly, to communicate more effectively with one another, let alone learn how to recognize and build up our good presentational points. Others hardly ever tell us, except in anger or irritation when judgements are clouded, what habits we have that are a total switch-off. Even those of us who are fluent, in that our words flow out, have to ask ourselves whether we convey an adequate, impressive or effective message. In normal conversation, after all, we speak on average seven times faster than we write. We have an innate process that quickly marshals our thoughts and words in an orderly manner before we subject others to them. These words, strung together properly, may make general sense, but surely we should allocate proportionately more time during our lives to improving the manner and not just the order in which they emerge? Everyone has some experience of some serious mis-understanding in their personal history where the words they used and the way they delivered them not only undervalued them but also distorted what they had really meant to say.

Body language, which in most interpersonal situations amounts to as much as half of the total message, plus paralanguage – the power, the gravitas, the cadences, the general magnetism of the voice – means that in casual or persuasive conversation, between workmates, between social partners and so on, the degree of attention depends to a large extent on non-verbal aspects of communication. Someone who stands tall, who radiates enthusiasm and competence, who has a certain personal magnetism, will be listened to more intently than others. We know from our places of work, that good managers get good results and bad managers, even though the work may be intrinsically fascinating, gain very little attention. Likewise, when we listen to an after-dinner speaker, we know within the first few moments or so whether we are going to pay attention or switch off and reach for the port. None of this is to do with content, but with the way the person comes to stand at the podium, and the manner in which contact is made with the audience. Even the way he or she dresses will have its effect on the audience. The matter of how people dress is taken too seriously by some and not seriously enough by others. For the purposes of your own Primacy Effect, it is a subject that is worth looking at in some detail.

Does Dress Matter?

While Oscar Wilde was being partly frivolous when he wrote 'A well-tied tie is the first serious step in life', Henry David Thoreau's remark that 'It is an interesting question how far men would retain their relative rank if they were divested of their clothes', deserves careful thought. By our clothes are we known.

Without your clothes, who are you?

Someone shabbily or inadequately dressed with a loud tie, or a woman with too much of a plunging neckline, will, by these distractions, seriously dilute the attention the audience gives them. The 'reading' of dress in all its forms is a very neglected subject, though we all recognize, for example, that the law, in the form of a policeman, dresses up in uniform to arrest a criminal, just as justice is administered by a judge wearing wig and robes. Such uniforms, such regalia, some of it redolent with history, is a deliberate social device that has been retained to impart awe and reverence, and a sense of the discipline and majesty of authority. In times past the same was true of teachers and professors who decked themselves out in their mortar-boards and gowns, which were worn to add dignity and to make the wearer better listened to if not better understood. These are not, of course, the only reasons for the wearing of uniforms or conforming dress: discipline, ease of identification, conformity and other factors all come into the argument. Equally, it is not just for hygienic reasons that doctors and nurses in a hospital have a certain dress code. Parking meter attendants and soldiers will, in different circumstances, be given a great deal of attention by us because of what they are wearing. In less formal circumstances we would probably not expect to see a male lawyer intent on defending our interests wearing a T-shirt and jangling earrings, any more than we might expect, say, an architect or a pop star to go around wearing a stiff collar and three-piece suit all the time.

Ease, convenience and comfort tend to play a part in how we dress. Utility often overrides style and even fashion. A shell-suit and trainers are all many of us really need. But dress in all its forms gives off strong messages. What does a man wearing a (non-formal) bow-tie say to you? What about jeans with knee holes in them, or someone wearing an Armani suit, or what has been called Oxfam chic? Even young people have their own uniforms or dress codes, often enforced by peer group pressure – flowing skirts, bare midriffs, body jewellery, thick socks, Nike trainers or Doc Marten boots. Dress proclaims the person, said Shakespeare, and while it would be absurd to force the conventionality of a suit, collar and tie or the female equivalent on everyone, an awareness of what you wear and how you wear it when you meet your various audiences is another essential part of the communication process. It was interesting, incidentally, to read recently how many designer-dressed pupils criticized their teachers for their 'sixties to eighties scruff' clothes. Compare this to President Jimmy Carter, who gave his famous fireside chats to the American people while wearing a woolly cardigan, prompting the man in the street, who wanted the President to look like a president, to ask, 'Who the hell does he think he is?'

It is not just what you wear but how you wear it that counts. While 'power dressing' may be a gimmicky expression, and few jobs require that you go through a daily military inspection, the little details – shoes polished, collars and cuffs clean, clothes pressed and crease free – can make the difference between success and rejection. Remember that a narrow-cut shirt with buttons straining round an overweight midriff (one advert for a Jermyn Street shop currently reads: 'You'll never get a job in a shirt like that!'), a stained and badly knotted tie, a skirt length that is out of keeping with the shape of the legs below – all these are details to beware. Remember that while fashion changes, style remains. Floppy bow-ties, ill-fitting suits, dirty shirt cuffs, suede shoes, two-tone shoes, flares, button-down shirts, coloured braces, too much colour co-ordination, too much costume jewellery, too much make-up, long sideburns, a soupstrainer moustache . . . What do these have in common? They are all things I personally over the years have heard criticized by my fellow interviewers.

Despite that, there are a number of public figures who are notable for having got away with their rather wayward dress sense. The well-known businessman John Harvey-Jones, even when he appeared on television, always seemed to have had his clothes thrown on him with a pitchfork. His ties had a tendency to hang at half-mast and his suits looked baggy and unpressed. The brilliant former British Ambassador to Washington, Sir Nicholas Henderson, despite his high-powered representational role, always looked as if he had been sleeping in his expensively cut suits. Gordon Brown, the Chancellor of the Exchequer, seems to appear everywhere, both in public and in social life, wearing the same business suit. His decision not to wear black tie at a grand City dinner was much frowned upon, while that same pinstripe outfit is sported even when he is watching a rugby match. The former Labour leader, Michael Foot, has gone down in history not for his leadership or public speaking skills (he had, when speaking, an ability never to seem to come to the end of a sentence) but for his appearance at the Cenotaph wreath-laying on Remembrance Day wearing, instead of a tailcoat or suitably sombre suit, a very battered donkey jacket. Michael Grade, the formidable former head of Channel 4 Television, is known for his flamboyant red braces and garishly matching red socks, just as Martin Bell, the former BBC war correspondent, who spent so much time in war-torn Bosnia and is now an Independent MP, is known for always wearing an off-white suit, even in very dangerous circumstances. That suit undoubtedly marked him out not just as a brave or foolish man, but as someone who could, with sincerity, talk about honesty and integrity in political life. His symbolic dress was a visual throwback to all the old Wild West movies where the cowboy hero always wore a white hat and rode, if possible, a white stallion. Most of the rest of us all have our little trademarks of dress, though we are not always fully aware of them.

Looking the Part

We like our business leaders to look the part. We do not expect them to dress like tailors' dummies, but we presume they will live up to their station in life. Chains and robes of office do not appear daily in most people's lives, but circumstances also dictate the appropriate dress codes. When we see government ministers being interviewed in their gardens or in their living-rooms over a crisis-laden weekend, we don't mind them being dressed in casual, open-necked shirts or sweaters. But as party conference organizers have long recognized, if someone comes to the podium expecting to be listened to with a degree of attentiveness, but without having dressed up for the occasion at least to some degree (and even in Communist China there is a precise dress code, if only the Mao tunic), it will be difficult for their message to get through.

A certain sense of colour-coding comes naturally to most of us. We know what suits us and when we should wear what. Dark suits we tend to equate with seriousness and trustworthiness, while light colours match relaxed occasions. Most of us also instinctively know how to dress to suit our characters, how to have style without being flash. We avoid designer clothes if we wish to avoid appearing too opulent or ostentatious; a high-quality style, however defined, for both men and women, may give an impression of slightly old-fashioned staidness, but there is, in most situations, advantage in tending towards the conservative. And classic style costs less in the long run, if only because it gets out of date less quickly than the latest fashion trend.

But what is style? The Beatles, the Princess of Wales, and designers like Sir Terence Conran have injected various styles into our national consciousness in one form or another over the years. Fashion changes, skirt lengths and things like body jewellery may come and go, but classic elegance remains. To sum up, clothes, as much as bearing and demeanour, are powerful, unspoken ways of communicating. It is not just what you wear but how you wear it that counts. Good, well-cut clothes and a matching, characterful way of speaking that grips an audience; these things are all to do with style. If you have it and know it, you win out over an opposition that does not.

Hair and Style

A word about hairstyles. You don't need the advertisers on television, who use up a huge amount of money (along with dogfood it is one of the most heavily advertised commodities) promoting their hair care products, to tell you how much attention this and most other societies give to hair quality. Hair and sexuality are constantly paraded together across our screens, where the message seems to be: get one right and you get the other. We unconsciously mark down some people's qualities because we are taken aback by their hairstyles. Contemporary American studies show that male politicians with short, neat hairstyles and no facial hair are, irrespective of party, much more trusted by the electorate. We recognize the various types:

- the Einstein, mad-professor cut
- the Old Etonian, nanny-brushed, immaculate parting, brushed hard down each side
- The 'I'm not bald because I've still got ten strands plastered across my skull' approach
- The US Marine bristle brush
- The millennium pudding-bowl style

- The 'I'm perpetually young' jet black 65-year-old, with a tiny show of illusionary grey at the temples
- The Nancy Reagan 'hairsprayed so much it'll break if you fall over' look
- The peroxide, suicide, dyed-by-her-own-hand blonde with the shabby dark roots
- and a thousand others.

Whether you believe Samson and Delilah's castration theory about hair length, a dramatic change in hairstyle (male or female) can signal a surprising amount in terms of message. Cherie Blair, the UK Prime Minister's wife, learned the hard way when she went to the States, taking with her her own special hairdresser. It was a perfectly reasonable thing to do, but it looked bad in the image stakes, since hair is always a superficially trivial yet intrinsically interesting subject to which the media like to draw attention. Think how many column inches were devoted to the late Princess of Wales's various hairstyles over the years. Michael Portillo's changing coiffure and Michael Heseltine's flowing locks have had more written about them at times than many of the serious issues with which they were concerned. Whether John Major's hairstyle was kept in place with a vast amount of hair gel, whether the current young Tory leader has any hair, and Tony Blair's attempts to hide his expanding bald patches, have all been subjects for much derided but still very public discussion. We may laugh, but we should draw the consequent lesson from these public figures and realize that our own hairstyles do say a surprising amount about us as well.

Then there are beards. Margaret Thatcher was said never to trust a man in a beard because either there was something too Bohemian trying to get out or he was trying to hide more than a weak chin. And as for long sideburns ... The tabloids had great fun when the left-wing Labour MP, Ken Livingstone, after two and a half decades, shaved off his moustache. They went for the easy joke that it was the only thing that had made his face memorable. But it made people concentrate on the extent to which facial hair has a genuine effect on our perception of others. Would we see Gerry Adams and Richard Branson differently if they were deprived of their facial growths? I knew an Ambassador in the Diplomatic Service many years ago who had a spade beard which made him look rather like an old Dutch sea-captain. It stuck out very aggressively and, despite the fact that he was a very mild-mannered man, the impression of constant confrontation branded him wherever he went. Beards can be reassuring and kindly if they are of the Santa Claus variety, but when one sees the Foreign Secretary, Robin Cook, or Alan Sugar the businessman on television, their beards bristling as they face the questioning of a hostile audience, their facial hair affects the judgements we make of their abilities and character.

Were they producing a film for television or for the cinema, Central Casting would probably not select Robin Cook, with his unshaven squirrel look, to play the role of a British Foreign and Commonwealth Secretary. He is not in the physical mould of the great figures who have led the Foreign Office in the past. Well aware of his looks, he has been quoted as saying that they would always have got in the way if he had ever had any thought of standing for the Labour leadership. On the other hand, Robin Cook presumably knows his own face and realizes what he looks like without his beard. And what about adding moustaches to our foremost leaders? Would we trust Mr Blair more with an RAF moustache, or would the leader of the opposition look older if he wore, or was able to grow, a heavy beard?

A word about perception, image, the Primacy Effect and spectacles. We have all seen the advertisements where beautiful women are put into horn-rimmed glasses (and optional white coats), thereby instantly becoming high-flying scientists or doctors. In Cambodia, such an association between spectacles and intelligence actually became a matter of life and death under Pol Pot's murderous regime. Thousands of people who wore glasses were put to death at the time of the so-called Killing Fields merely for being suspected of being intellectuals, and thus seen as enemies of that evil dictator.

Spectacles, if worn as a fashion accessory, can have a positive effect, can be attractive and sexy, but can equally be a turn-off and can, if badly chosen and worn, impede eye contact with any audience. It is therefore important, if you wear spectacles, to choose the right shape and frame. Do you look best in a heavy horn-rimmed affair or something light, even frameless? Do you choose frames that go up at the edges to accentuate the shape of the eyebrows, or do you go for the round, earnest, schoolboy look? Take much more time and advice next time. Go into your optician's, and look at yourself long and hard with a variety of different frames on your face, starting with the more extreme ones, from the Dame Edna Everage glitzy through to the wired-on National Health Service ones, and see how much that simple facial accoutrement changes the entire impression you give. Above all, seek advice. Spectacles can be great, but I have seen at interviews and presentations how they can also be a real barrier between you and the rest of the world.

Proxemics

Apart from body language, dress and all that, an important factor in whether you pay attention to someone is how close you stand to them, what is called *proxemics*. If you are too far away from someone, you will have to raise your voice or you will not be heard and may not gain the necessary degree of attention. Equally, if you stand too close to people (halitosis apart), they may register their disapproval by concentrating their attention on trying to keep their distance rather than on what you are saying. Body space, which is the amount of territory we like to work in, should be respected: it is all too easy to intrude or to fake intimacy by crossing the threshold into too close a zone, one reserved only for the most intimate of relationships. Tests suggest that in Western society, if you come within eighteen inches of someone when you are not intimate, then you are being unreasonably intrusive. Practical research shows that a business colleague or stranger should stand at least four feet away, but a distance of up to twelve feet is even more correct. Other evidence shows that northern Europeans stand much further apart in normal social intercourse than those from around the Mediterranean. The latter also tend to use their hands more, touching each other to register or emphasize a point. It is not too dissimilar to the familiarity of your facial language; the eyes, the smiles, the frowns, the grimaces, the attentiveness with which the person talking or being talked to catches and holds on to a look, can suggest either too much familiarity or remoteness. On the television screen, newsreaders gain the attention of their audience by staring straight at the camera as they read from the in-built teleprompt, but in a one-to-one situation, if you try to go eyeball to eyeball all the time, you will, unless you are on very intimate terms, almost certainly make your interlocutor uneasy.

Talking with the Hands

As Freud pointed out, hand movements give away so much. Slow, methodical, open-handed gestures, used to emphasize a point, can come across with enormous power and effect. Nervous fiddling with rings or with fingers, however, can do an unexpected degree of damage with someone who is watching out for such tell-tale signs. In certain controlled situations, hands can give themselves away by not doing anything. Criminologists have shown that when people are lying or cheating, they will make every effort to reduce the number of hand movements to avoid revealing their anxieties.

Kipling once wrote: 'Words are the most powerful drug used by mankind.' We know that to be true. But we also know people who have no gift for languages – not even their own. It does not stop many of them saying nothing, badly and at length. Equally we know people who have voices of authority, resonance and charm. Many radio and TV presenters, in the John Humphries, Alastair Cooke tradition, are chosen for their clarity of diction and the overall 'listenability' of their speech patterns, as are those comfortable, confident voices which are hired by the advertising media to persuade us to buy something or other. We mostly manage, in day-to-day speech, to speak in modulated cadences, stressing some words and pausing for dramatic effect. We raise or lower our voices depending on the message and the emphasis we seek to give. Above all, we try to time our words for best effect. Some people have good in-built paralanguage; others have not. John Major, when he tried to speak with authority, only sounded, as Matthew Parris has written, as if he was trying to imitate Mystic Meg. By contrast, Michael Heseltine, even when his content was sparse, could hold even a hostile audience with his oratory.

When we speak we adjust to the audience we have, reacting to the feedback we receive, all those small clues that tell us if the other person has understood, welcomed or rejected what we have said. If they look puzzled or blank, we know we have to say more. If they sit upright and alert and intent, or lean towards us rather than avoiding our gaze, we may have their attention. If they slouch, seemed bored, or stare vacantly out of the window, we are probably going to have to spice up our act. If they smile in response to our message, this, in itself, is usually a positive sign.

Words and Meaning

Forget paralanguage for a moment and look at pure, unadorned language. It is all you need, with unencumbered, unaccentuated words, to communicate certain straightforward facts or messages like when a train is due to leave a station. You are able to do so because, unless you are speaking a foreign language, each word normally has a commonly understood meaning. It is particularly easy when those words are simple ones like 'table' or 'bed' or 'ten o'clock'. (It becomes more difficult with complex terms such as 'infinity' or 'the human spirit' or 'love'.) You automatically decode the words or combination of words that others use. Such 'pure' language is all you need for passing on basic information or news. The long-suffering person who recorded the British Telecom speaking clock did not need to inject too much drama into 'At the third stroke, the time sponsored by ...', nor does it need emotion to read out the latest stock market figures.

Between close relatives or friends, a few incomprehensible or half-formed words can be sufficient to communicate a hugely important message. A simple admonition like 'you're late' can have a whole range of meanings, depending on whether it is delivered with fury, with resignation or with a tolerant smile. Bernard Shaw once said that the way to tell a true Englishman was to see if he could say 'really' in a dozen different ways, but here intonation and emphasis come back into play. When you are operating in extremely familiar situations, for example in a company where people have worked together for a long time and everyone is familiar with both the business and the individuals involved, the communication process can become drastically foreshortened. Then a lot of verbal shorthand, so-called 'Company Chinese', is increasingly used, as in *'JD's wild on the top list item, though the old man'll go you know how if PK's not up to speed with his info ...'* You do not need to spell out every detail of what or whom you are talking about; it is equally well known to the listener. You develop codes and other keys which, to an outsider, if not totally incomprehensible, are at best partially disguised. It is rather like picking up the look between two people who are strangers to you. To you, an outside observer, that glance may appear threatening or hostile. You may be right but you don't know for certain: the participants may just be acting out some intimate, innocent joke. While on the subject of reading other people's paralanguage and gestures, we do that all the time, without ever waiting to eavesdrop. Travelling on the tube the other day I watched as two Russians – it sounded Russian, though I don't speak it – argued over some document they were both reading. I didn't understand a word, but I 'read' a great deal of what they were talking about and even more about the degree of their mutual hostility. Their body and paralanguage spoke volumes.

From childhood on, as we learn to speak, we recognize other visual and tonal clues to meaning. We will 'read' when our parents are angry or pleased. As adults, we add human interaction: we don't just say 'eat your food' to a baby in a high chair; we mime the process in the hope of encouraging a sometimes very messy imitation. By this mix of words and gestures we get our message across. Watch a television drama with the sound turned down and you will probably get some of the flavour of the plot. Watch two people talking at a distance and, even if you can only hear the muted sounds of their voices and not the words, you may still be able to pick up a little of what is going on between them.

Just as facial expressions will tell you things about happiness, sadness, surprise, disgust or contempt, so if you attempt to voice your views in a dull monotone and try to keep your face totally emotionless, not only will you be very boring but your message is far less likely to get through. Psychological studies have demonstrated again and again how important a lively paralanguage is in putting yourself across to others. To emphasize the point, one such study, carried out in 1972, looked at what happened when people were given a verbal message in a non-verbal style that actually contradicted the message – for example, given bad news by someone wearing a wide grin. The results showed that the non-verbal cues had about five times the effect as the verbal ones. If people were given a friendly message in a hostile manner, it was not the words that they took note of, remembered or acted upon, but the looks. Thus we all take particular care how we appear, or smile, or look concerned, if we feel some delicate message might be taken the wrong way. That 1972 study again confirmed that out of the three parts of the message – body and facial expressions, tone of voice and words – the words were consistently the *least* important of all.

To conclude, the average person (if such exists) is reputed, when engaged in everyday social and business life, to use about 30,000 words per day. These words are as nothing compared with the sight of a trembling hand which, like a clenched fist, a wink or a seductive smile, can speak volumes to the listener.

'So what else is wrong with my posture, my body language, my communicating skills?' asked Bill, crossly. 'I've thrown away that tie and have bought *two* replacements – one that screams conformity and the other ... freedom.' He was forcing himself to keep control because JD, the Chairman, was silently watching this particular exchange with Ruth Mackenzie. 'Explain more,' he added. 'Why d'you think this non-verbal communication business is so important?'

'You've observed people over the years, Bill,' came her reply. 'A lot of them don't get the attention they deserve because of certain nasty habits, body tick, mannerisms, slovenly ways of speaking. Agreed?'

Bill's own body language showed that he was still far from convinced, but he nodded reluctantly.

'OK. Look at it this way,' Ruth Mackenzie continued. 'You go down to the pub and someone tells a joke. You know perfectly well that the same joke told by an expert – like you, Bill – can have everybody falling around holding their sides, while someone else laboriously spelling out exactly the same words will cause the joke to fall flat on its face.'

'All right,' said Bill with a sigh. 'Say, mentioning pubs, how d'you feel about a quick ...' he looked across at JD, who frowned, so Bill shrugged and walked over to the windows with his hands clasped behind his back.

'That's a splendid piece of acting, Bill.' Ruth smiled. 'Rejected so dejected. Your whole body is shrieking. A bit like a small schoolboy who has been ticked off, if you don't mind me saying so.'

Bill turned round, then grinned unexpectedly. 'Maybe I'm beginning to grasp the point,' he said.

'Believe it or not, some psychologists have even researched joke-telling. The laughter depends much less on the subject matter than on the three magic ingredients of the comedian's trade: long pauses, fluctuations in intonation, which means paralanguage to you and me, and clever gestures. Any serious comedian guides the audience by using those non-verbal signals.' She paused, realizing she was again beginning to antagonize him.

'OK, OK. Comedy is a serious business,' said Bill. He was starting to sulk again.

'If you'll excuse us, JD. Maybe we'd better loosen up both our body languages by going off for a quick drink,' said Ruth Mackenzie, getting to her feet. 'On the way down to the pub maybe I'll pick up one of those greeting cards that has a chip with an electronic laugh built into it. You know the sort of thing. Then I'll bore you all about how scientists have deduced from the amused reaction that most people give to hearing even an electronic chortle, that laughter is unconsciously controlled.'

'God almighty,' said Bill, grinning again. 'Make mine a double.'

PERSONAL ASSESSMENT REPORT: CASE STUDY NO. 2

PERSONAL AND CONFIDENTIAL REPORT BY MS CONSULTANTS (EXECUTIVE SEARCH) REQUESTED FOR CLIENT A

Given that you are now 57 and the fact that, despite being strongly tipped to get the last major job, you failed to do so and have also been runner-up in competition for three other senior positions over the last half-year, you asked me for a personal, written assessment of what has been going wrong. Some of what I have to say may appear brutally frank, but this, I am afraid, is what is required if you are to get another senior post before you retire.

I have explained to you that the facts about yourself, your CV, the letters from referees and so on are never enough. They are good; some are outstanding, but these facts need help. Each of the candidates on any shortlist we put up to clients is perfectly capable of doing the job on offer; we would not be doing *our* job if that was not the case. Thus clients, when they get on shortlists, tend to ignore those CVs and go for appearances, how you come into the room, how you sit at the table, what you do with your hands, how you speak, whether you look at the questioner, and a lot more besides. If you think that is trivial stuff, think again. You, I'm sorry to say, failed on a whole number of these counts, and they all stack up. As a matter of urgency, therefore, we strongly advise you to go about getting some help on the self-presentation front. I saw you just before the final interview and, if you don't mind me saying so, that light-weight, off-fawn suit may be very comfortable, but it is hardly the thing that top people wear these days. My guess is that alone, and you had obviously travelled in it that morning, so it could have done with an iron – I hear your growl of anger – was not a minor part in your downfall.

Forgive me for saying so but facial hair – in your case that splendid RAF moustache – has a strongly adverse effect on a lot of people. That, coupled with your half-moon glasses which are always perched half-way down your nose, reminds some people of a half-forgotten character actor who played benevolent roles, but that is hardly the image you want to give to hard-headed businessmen in today's world.

I strongly recommend you, costly though it can be, to have a day or so's training with a professional coach. You know what you want to say, and you don't say it too badly, though you tend to address people in an avuncular, genial, laid-back style, but the overall impression you give (you've admitted you have put on a lot of weight recently, so maybe, unless you've got the willpower to take it off, buying a slightly larger suit might be a good investment) is of being a bit tired and past it. I know that you are not, you know that you are not. Make sure the rest of the world doesn't think you are slipping into life-has-passed-me-by mode. Show yourself to be as vigorous and sparky as I know you can be.

Sorry about all the above. It is up to you from now on, then let us have another chat.

CHAPTER 4

Getting Through to People

They see you and hear you, but do they listen?

How to improve your performance

As a vessel is known by the sound, whether it be cracked or not, so men are proved by their speeches whether they be wise or foolish.

Demosthenes

When ideas fail, words come in very handy.
Goethe

The manner of you speaking is fully as important as the matter, as more people have ears to be tickled than understandings to judge.

Lord Chesterton

A man's style is his mind's voice.
Ralph Waldo Emerson

What you sound like is what you are. The way you speak more than the words you use marks you down as someone who should be listened to. Tone of voice, clarity, accent, the whole package of paralanguage defines you more than any other single factor in your entire make-up. You can change the degree of resonance and authority with which you speak, and can do so with ease. To begin with, use a tape recorder or a mirror with memory – a video camera – and really listen to how you sound at present.

Few of us make much of an effort to adjust what we are saying to whom we are talking. If you make a statement at a dinner table with seven other guests, there may be up to seven different opinions and attitudes both to you and to the views you have expressed. The same is true in all areas of life. You need to spend time not only on what you intend to say and how you say it, but also to whom you are saying it. What may be a devastatingly conclusive or effective argument to one may be anathema to another.

You cannot join the AA after your car has broken down any more than you can first insure yourself with BUPA from your hospital bed. So it is with image building. You ought to do it before you need it.

You can hear someone talking in the next room, but it does not mean that they can hear you. As I said earlier, you probably learned to speak around the ages of two to three, but have you made much of an attempt to listen to, or improve on, how you sound since then? Unless you are one of the few people who take elocution lessons, probably not. Why is it that you spend so much time and effort in acquiring many other skills and qualifications yet ignore the means of communicating with other people? Again and again, the mumblers and mutterers of life get cast aside because they are just that. The British Labour Party before the last election recognized that fact and put a number of their front-bench team on a weekend crash course to improve their leadership and communication skills. (It later leaked out that the ebullient and blunt John Prescott, the future Deputy Prime Minister, was not invited, though when challenged on this he briskly explained, 'Everybody already understands my body language' – a fact that is difficult to dispute.)

Hammering the message home

Self Assessment

If you are not John Prescott and not too set in your ways, what do you do about improving your performance? First and foremost, sit down quietly and make a truthful personal assessment of how you perform at the moment. With a video or tape recorder, read out some piece of text or make an impromptu speech or presentation about something that you're very familiar with. Do it in private, then play it back, listening carefully, not so much to the words or the 'ums' and 'ers' (they are easily got rid of), but to *how* you say what you have to say. How do you judge the texture of your own voice? What would you mark it out of ten, from resoundingly compelling to bumblingly incoherent? Of course you will not be able to do this objectively, but it is a start. After that, you need outside help.

Getting Help

The next step, if you are serious about improving, is to get some external, preferably professional assistance. It is not just public figures who need communications guidance, or who benefit from 'buying image'. Get someone you can trust to give you a tough, one-off, no-holds-barred assessment of how you stand, dress, speak, convince. It will really be value for money. Ask yourself, then ask them:

- Am I believable?
- Am I coherent?
- Do people listen to me?
- If not, why not?
- What am I good at?

- What am I poor at?
- Do I look the part?
- If not, why not?

I would strongly recommend *not* asking a close relative or friend to do all this. No matter how splendidly wise and kind they are, they are bound to come with too many in-built hang-ups or favourable prejudices about you. No matter how honest you and they think they are being, they will not tell you the real truth if they think it is going to hurt you too much or spoil a beautiful friendship. Most modern business and political leaders take independent advice like this, even the most unexpected ones. Newly revealed Cabinet Papers show that even thirty years ago Harold Wilson had a voice coach, Cicily Berry, who told him to keep his utterances short, sharp and simple. We all came to know later about how the machiavellian people that flitted in and out of the anterooms of power during the Thatcher administration, Charles Powell, Bernard Ingham, Tim Bell, Gordon Reece and others, all advised her on her image and style. In today's environment any top captain of industry will have a Peter Mandelson hidden somewhere on the company payroll, helping them with the window-dressing of their personal and corporate affairs, and otherwise managing the public's illusions about them.

Accent – Does it Matter?

The next step is to get any hang-ups you may have about accent out of the way. You were born with a certain accent. Whether or not to upgrade it, for example to so-called Standard English, is a personal choice for you to make. Contemporary life is littered with people – politicians, actors, broadcasters, lawyers – who have had their accents altered as a result of a change of residence, or have done so deliberately in the belief that it will help them get on. It is not just in British society – try and get on in the United States or Germany or France with a strong regional accent – that prejudice of the type Professor Higgins defined is still far from dying out. As soon as you open your mouth, others will categorize you. There is plenty of recruitment

agency evidence to show conclusively that a very strong accent negatively affects your employment prospects in many areas of activity.
There are crude prejudices out there, which, acting on the basis of
instant impressions, still mark down a heavy accent as some bastard
form of the 'norm'. The plaintive, complaining, nasal English of the
former European Community leader, Jacques Delors, prejudiced many
people, and not just the tabloid readers in Britain, against everything
he was saying. Because he sounded whingeing, because he always
seemed to speak negatively about what was going on, the good sense
he often talked went unnoticed.

Many people with strong regional or class accents do not realize
how noticeable they are until they move out of their region or class.
In metropolitan London and the South-East of England, even if the
individual speaks grammatically and with precision and clarity, some
accents will be acceptable, some decidedly not. Big companies with
large numbers of telephone enquiry or sales staff, after a great deal of
research, have set up in towns like Leeds or Glasgow – both surprising
locations to some – since these accents are held to travel reasonably
well. But generally what is acceptable in one place goes unrespected
elsewhere. A very upper-class English accent, for example, can go
down extremely badly in urban Scotland, often to the point of serious
hostility. By contrast, the General Medical Council, helped by the
television dramatists and their Central Casting colleagues, who always
seem to opt for north-of-the-border medical characters, recently
debated whether having a Scottish accent helped make you a more
believable doctor in real life. Certainly there are a disproportionate
number of Scots in the top echelons of the medical profession, but
that probably has more to do with the historic quality of the medical
schools in Scotland than with accent.

If one listens to wartime broadcasts or the parodies of them used in
some current advertising where everyone speaks in highly accented,
upper-class English, it helps underline the fact that, in Britain and
North America, there still are authoritative voices, such as those used
in the BBC's Radio 4 news bulletins, which are believed to be better
at informing the world about hard news in a totally dispassionate way.

Anyone who remembers hearing the former German Chancellor,
Willi Brandt, speaking English, which he did in a strong, deep and
gravelly voice, and, incidentally, in much less accented English than

his contemporary, the then American Secretary of State, Henry Kissinger, whose Germanic accent was very pronounced, will also remember how compelling and authoritative it sounded. Willi Brandt, in the words of veteran British Labour politician Dennis Healey, always spoke sense because he *sounded* as if he was speaking sense. Healey himself is another good example of this. His voice tones travel well across the world. He is respected, now if not always in a long political career, largely for the way he says what he has to say, the humour, wit and liveliness of his voice tones carrying his argument.

It was always said that many Americans did not believe the daily news on television unless the distinguished American anchorman Walter Cronkite read it. With his grizzled appearance, his well-cut grey moustache and his overall resonance, he spoke with a voice of authority about everything that happened. It was he, largely, who managed to get the famous Camp David Agreement up and running. People listened to him because they liked him and because they believed that, no matter what he read out, it was the truth and nothing but the truth. Today there are few other broadcasters like him, though Alistair Cooke is another whose voice has spanned many decades in bringing, with wit and candour, the message about the ways and wisdoms of one country to another.

To the surprise of some, Walter Cronkite said to me on one occasion that Sir David Frost was one of the best practitioners of the interviewer's art. Frost is frequently criticized for what appears to be a somewhat ingratiating form of interview, but the man who once interviewed the Shah of Persia, and made Nixon cry, has a remarkable ability to extract information and, because of the apparent gentleness of his questioning, to elicit responses which the politicians and others whom he interviews in his weekly programmes, frequently come to regret. With hardnosed, abrasive interviewers, these public figures are on their guard. With this gentle, easy approach, their defences fall.

Many leading politicians, businessmen and women, churchmen, commissioned members of the armed forces, along with those budding actors and actresses at their drama schools, try to emulate strong, authoritative vowel sounds to make themselves more listenable to. Some young lawyers intending to go to the Bar actually take elocution lessons to imitate voices that are perceived as successful in the top echelons of judicial life. Not all of this can be blamed on some dreadful hangover from the class system. It is a fact of life that certain voices grate, and while social voice-changing may be seen as hypocritical, even your standard bishop is expected to sound 'right', since an over-accented voice from the pulpit would fail to convince. Finally, like it or not, some academic studies have demonstrated that a good, clear, Standard English accent suggests, as an adjunct to the Halo Effect, a higher degree not only of education, but of management and other leadership skills as well. Persistent use of local varieties of English, particularly if they come complete with regionalized expressions, will be a serious handicap outside an individual's own community. Many people get round this by doing what is technically known as Code Switching – adjusting in and out of Standard English depending on their audience: at home they will speak as they always used to; in the workplace they will quickly adapt to the norms of their new environment. There is nothing unusual about this. As any teacher will recognize, the language of the classroom and of the playground can be very different indeed.

The Video: a Mirror with Memory

Having decided what you are going to do about your accent – and the best advice is often to leave it alone – the next thing is to be absolutely certain of how you are heard and seen by others. Making a video recording of yourself speaking, talking, conversing, having a mock interview with a friend, delivering a short speech or whatever, and then concentrating on not so much the words but how you look and how you say what you have to say, will take you a long way. Next, turn the sound right down and, remembering some of the points made in previous chapters about the Primacy Effect, have a good critical look at how you stand and dress and what your hand movements and body language look like without the distractions of the sound. With the sound up again, and bearing in mind the mark you have given yourself out of ten in terms of tone of voice, authority, and so on, try to look at each aspect in turn and see what you think you need to change. That crumpled suit? That frightful shirt? That hairstyle? That skirt length? That slouched posture? Those mumbled cadences? All of these will have to be tackled one by one.

In all this I am not advocating that you become like those young actors and actresses I mentioned above who are deliberately taught to be able to become what and whom they are not. They make a living out of convincing us by using many different skills, accents, voice patterns and other non-verbal devices. Your job is to convince, not by being devious or by acting out some part, but by fielding your best attributes properly. It is all about looking at yourself, brutally frankly, then isolating and identifying your own downside and unique selling points.

Even people in the public eye get it wrong. The papers are full of stories of people communicating foolishly or badly and being torn apart as a result. There was some correspondence in *The Times* last year commenting on the absurd and somewhat demeaning habit of corporate leaders posing for photographers, usually in highly artificial circumstances, in order to illustrate some piece of news or non-news: annual results, a take-over, the announcement of a new contract and so on. The resulting pictures tend to come out like second-rate PR shots, with chairman or chief executives of utility companies looking uncomfortable as they drink refreshingly unpolluted glasses of tap water, or airline bosses surrounded by glamorous air hostesses smiling broadly even when the corporate news is grim. It is the standard newspaper equivalent of the TV journalist desperately trying to add visual impact to a story by standing shivering in the rain outside some anonymous office, government department or factory door. It is intended to add the human touch to dull business stories. It seldom works. Shareholders are certainly not impressed, nor are the rest of us. The point about this aside is to underline the fact that if you are going to parade yourself for some reason, you should first look very carefully at what your image says about you and what you hope to achieve.

Just as Richard Burton was said to be able to read from a telephone directory and make it sound like great drama, so politicians generally acquire skills in advocating policies in which they privately may have little faith. Defence lawyers, equally, are trained to argue cases in which they 'sell' their client's innocence to an impressionable jury, even though they do not believe it themselves. Whatever the ethics of treating a jury not as an arbiter of justice, but as an audience as if at a play, we are all guilty, as we saw above, of 'putting on an act' to get a point across to a loved one or to a colleague. We feign or exaggerate amusement, or sorrow, or admiration, or anger, depending on the occasion. In major and in minor ways, even if we are very honest, we all occasionally dissemble in order to come a little closer to what we want to be seen to be. If you decide to act this way, for example when trying to push through a business deal, do it properly and rehearse, otherwise you can end with as much ham as a bad actor.

When you are next with a group of people, look at those around you for fifteen seconds, and then, trying to put out of your mind what you know about them, judge whether you are impressed by the way they present themselves. Look at their posture, observe how they appear, sit, stand and dress, and decide whether they inspire immediate confidence or exude charm or sincerity. Are *they* putting on an act? Are *they* pretending to be what they are not? Remember that you yourself will, despite your best endeavours, be guilty of stereotyping them because of their sex, race, age or what they are wearing. All these factors, taken together, will produce their effect on you, when they set out to convince, to advocate, to sell, to persuade. You will certainly reach the conclusion that those who look good and sound genuine do better than their colleagues. To misquote the late Lord Mancroft, 'We are all born equal, but quite a few of us get over it by working up our image.'

History is littered with people who have forced themselves to the top of the ladder as a result of some problem or slight they have suffered in their past. It was always said that Harold Macmillan only became the political leader he did on account of the discovery that his wife was having an affair with his erstwhile political friend Robert Boothby. Other people overcome physical handicaps to achieve success. Evelyn Glennie, the brilliant, internationally acclaimed percussionist, is profoundly deaf; David Blunkett, the UK's Education Secretary, has overcome his blindness with admirable fortitude; and there are numerous other examples in political and industrial life of people who have set out to overcome early adversity or poverty, or the lack of decent education, and prove to people from their past – parents, lovers, colleagues, enemies – that they could end up triumphant. You are fortunate if you have no inherited problems, but it should not stop you wanting to do your very best in the image stakes.

While we will look at specific skills in later chapters, there are many other things you can do from the outset to communicate more effectively. First and foremost, you have to identify your audience, what their interests are and why you should interest them. Even at a one-on-one level, you have got to inspire them to listen. They will, deep down, compare you to any opposition you have, and, as always in life, there is little to be said for being runner-up.

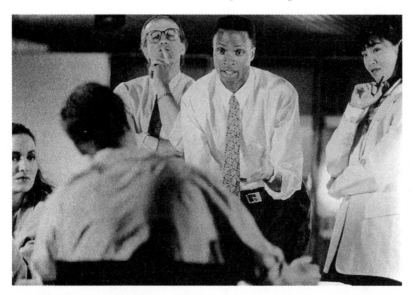

Are you getting the message across?

Then there is your message, whatever it is. We have all experienced people failing to sell themselves or their soap-powder for presentational reasons. But the quality of the actual message itself does matter too. Many of us try to make things too complex, too wordy, too long. Better to go for short, simple, sharp, bullet points or twenty-second sound-bites – my product is the best, my strategy is the winner – than a long-drawn-out ramble. If you are not convinced by your own rhetoric, why should they be?

Positives and Negatives

Among the positive and negative Primacy Effect factors that, in my experience, interviewers, recruitment specialists and headhunters as well as clients have identified are the items set out in the list below. Many of these points are so simple and so obvious that they seem hardly worth mentioning. Indeed, one critic of a previous book of mine on personal impact matters wrote that he did not need Michael Shea to tell him to dry his palms and brush the dandruff from his shoulders before a job interview. He was wrong. Many people do need just that. (I met my journalist critic much later. He was a walking health hazard and wrote from home since colleagues could not stand working beside him.)

Positive	Negative
Speaks clearly	Mutters
Stands tall	Slouches
Confident	Diffident
Firm handshake	Wet handshake
Good eyelock	Shifty-eyed/Never looked at us
Motivated	Didn't know what he/she wanted
Took the lead	Always had to be prompted
Well groomed	Scruffy
Intelligently curious	Disinterested
Well dressed	Carelessly dressed
Agreeable	Surly

Yes, they all look so obvious, spelled out here on the printed page. However, they are frequently overlooked by those entering the meeting or interview room. I have seen the evidence again and again and again.

To summarize, it is a question of first recognizing, then building on your existing strengths, and adding the key ingredients of confidence, poise and persuasiveness. It is not about simple image-making, but to do with that oft-repeated truth that perception is often the only reality others have to go on. In the next chapters we are going to look at certain special skills in the communications process. Even there I do not suggest that there is only one set of rules, one style of public speaking, one way to approach an interview. We all have to develop our own performance and pace. Making a good personal impact goes beyond merely putting on an act, but it is that as well.

No book can ever teach the interpersonal skills required to improve your impact on others, but it can provide a set of guidelines, and reveal the great but simple secret that *you can improve rapidly, and lastingly.* Hold up that mirror with memory, to see yourself as others see you. Look closely at that television monitor. In my long experience of teaching these personal impact skills, 75 per cent of what happens thereafter is self-learnt, as you come to see what you do well and what you do badly. There are a few gimmicks and, rather like riding a bicycle, the skills, once learnt, are never forgotten.

Communication is a two-way process. If you don't observe the behavioural courtesies and norms, if you don't use the correct social tools, especially in inter-gender or inter-age relationships, if you don't allow the other person to respond and have their say, or if you interrupt or are obviously not listening, it will be you that loses out in the end. Degrees of formality or informality exist within any group or in any company. If you misjudge the social or work environment in which you operate or hope to operate by upgrading it or downgrading it, then the pitfalls are obvious. It is not that you always need to conform, but if you are not conforming, be sure that you are aware of it. Manners, or codified manners which we call etiquette, exist even in the most casual environments. The rule here is, always err on the side of too much formality rather than too little. It's safer.

Telephone Communication

A small but important final point: when you are speaking on the telephone, just as when you hear someone on the radio, there is much less for you and the other party to go on in terms of the message being delivered. Where there is no visual element to the communication process, if you are trying to put a point across to a stranger, you need to use more paralanguage and speak with more built-in exclamation marks as it were, using more pitch and raising your voice at

Are you making the right connection?

the end when asking a question. You may also find that you need to give some indication of mood changes, like laughing audibly to indicate that you are being light-hearted, or sighing to demonstrate the reverse, something which your expressions would render unnecessary in face-to-face conversations. Some people have a good telephone voice and manner and some quite definitely do not. It's not just a matter of charm and glibness; in such circumstances you have to put more inflection and drama into your voice to make your point. Equally, you need to fill any sound gaps more: unless it is a very tense conversation, long silences are out, with pauses much shorter than in everyday speech, and not just in order to keep the phone bills down. 'Are you still there?' is a question usually delivered with anxiety or irritation because no confirmatory grunts have been coming from the other end of the line. In all other forms of communication, the 'pregnant pause' is an important point that we will return to later.

'How was that for you?' Bill asked provocatively. He felt quite elated as he left the lectern where he had just delivered a short presentation on the future strategy of the company for the sole benefit of Dr Mackenzie. He knew he hadn't lost his place and his hesitations had been minimal.

'Not bad,' she replied, cautiously. 'The content was good, as it ought to be from somebody in your position. So we can forget about the words.'

'That's the good news?' asked Bill, trying not to show his anxieties. The more he was brought face to face with his image, particularly by her, the less secure he felt.

'It is good news. The bad news is that while you were perfectly adequate and you didn't "um" and "er" too much, there's precious little drama in your voice. A normal audience would have gone to sleep after the first few minutes.'

'Thanks a package,' said Bill, scowling.

'You wanted the truth?' said Ruth Mackenzie. 'I repeat: you were very adequate.'

'I hate that word.'

'Which is why I chose it. You want to move on up from being just adequate. You need to make a quantum leap. You're perfectly capable of doing so. It all comes back to posture and paralanguage. You stood there, slouched over the lectern, reading from the text with no attempt at any eye-contact. Any audience would yawn and say "If he's just going to read to us, why the hell doesn't he give us the text, and let's go off for a good lunch." ' Ruth Mackenzie paused. 'I told you. Unless your text is a very complicated one, you should try and speak from notes. You know your subject perfectly: stand tall, which you did at the beginning, and you look really commanding, really good.'

'Wowee – was that a near-compliment?' asked Bill. 'What else? I might as well get all the bad news out of the way.'

'You're talking. But is the message getting through? You have the structure there, you've got the clarity, your accent in your case doesn't get in the way, but your body language is a zero. You look so disinterested in what you are saying. Try to build up a bit of rapport with your audience. Develop some eye-lock. Just remember what I said about the Primacy Effect. Any audience wants to like you. They want to respect you. But image wins. You have very little time. You're not given a second chance.'

'I've got the point,' growled Bill.

'You're coming along well. Quite a good pupil, really,' said Ruth Mackenzie, softly.

'Where does being patronizing and condescending fit into the Primacy Effect?' Bill asked suddenly, and Ruth had the good nature to smile.

MS CONSULTANTS
TRAINING PROGRAMME NO. 1

CANDIDATE: NEWLY APPOINTED CEO OF MAJOR PLC

CONFIDENTIAL BACKGROUND REPORT

The new appointee, aged 45, is taking over from a household name who has been frequently and prominently profiled in the business pages. He therefore has to make his mark, not out of a wish for self-publicity, but so that the City and the market see from the outset that the leadership of the Company is passing into competent hands. The problem is that the new CEO feels that he already projects perfectly adequately and believes that his record and that of the Company are all that asset managers and analysts need to go on. He is seriously hostile to any suggestion that he needs help and is only now prepared to accept some communications and public speaking training at the direct insistence of the Chairman and the Board of Directors.

REPORT

The CEO, obviously a successful and resourceful man, was, at the beginning of the training session, extremely negative. He did not need or want help from us over 'window-dressing' himself. (We could have reminded him that John Major also rejected, until too late, help with his image.) He reluctantly gave a short presentation and then a brief speech, both of which we recorded and played back to him. He declared that he was reasonably pleased with his performance, but doubts started to set in, particularly when we played the tape back once more with the sound turned right down and he was able to concentrate on how he looked, stood and dressed, without the immediate distraction of the words, on which, naturally, he had concentrated.

We gradually got a more reasonable dialogue going, when he himself began to volunteer that he needed a new suit, a decent haircut and to stop slouching over the lectern. We then played the tape a third time, on this occasion with the picture turned off, and he was able to concentrate on his paralanguage and especially the lack of any enthusiasm or drive in his voice. He said it: 'I am so boring!' We then set to work in a much more constructive and positive fashion.

RESULTS

The new CEO proved to be an excellent student and quickly and effectively picked up what he had been doing wrong. Almost from the outset he stood taller at the podium and put much more emphasis and enthusiasm into his voice. By the end of the day he was actually very pleased by what he had achieved, particularly when we played back the tape of his performance first thing in the morning in comparison with the final tape.

He left, bound for his tailors, to order a new suit, and has agreed to a follow-up session in the near future.

CHAPTER 5

Interview Skills

A prudent man must always follow in the footsteps of great men and imitate those who have been outstanding. If his own prowess fails to compare with theirs, at least it has an air of greatness about it.

Machiavelli

One man that has a mind and knows it, can always beat ten men who haven't and don't.

George Bernard Shaw

When a true genius appears in the world, you may know him by this sign, that the dunces are all in confederacy against him.

Jonathan Swift

A smile is when both corners of your mouth go up at the same time.
Vladimir Soloviev, teaching his Moscow course
on Western job-interviewing skills

Time Magazine once wrote that 'Greatness in the Presidential Chair islargely an illusion of the people'. Even if you are not aiming quite that high, it is still crucial to realize that when several candidates fora job, all with equally promising CVs, all with equal background experience and character references, are being interviewed, the one that presents him or herself and communicates best will come out on top.

Whatever side of the interview table you are sitting on, the person or people opposite have a very different agenda from you. As a candidate you want to give of your best. They want to make a judgement about you. You've got to try to get these two agendas to meet in the middle. They've got to rate you top.

A great deal of research has gone into looking at how people in authority, personnel managers, headhunters and human resource specialists choose whom they want. Can they ever be truly rational and dispassionate? Do they, the skills and experience of the various candidates being equal, tend to select people like themselves, or go for total opposites? Do they seek clones or people susceptible to cloning so as to create a working environment where everyone is like-minded and there will be fewer frictions? Or do they, as President John F. Kennedy was said to have done, deliberately select those who might well spar and bicker a bit, in the belief that such tensions are creative and that conflict can lead to more imaginative and constructive policy decisions in the long term? Given such possible prejudices, how far should anyone prepare for an interview, or is it all a bit of a waste of time?

The answer is that only a fool does not prepare him or herself well in advance. At the outset you have to be clear about what the interviewer is actually looking for. Do you really know? You have to be equally confident what *you* want. What are your goals? Who are you talking to? What's in it for both sides? Before you go near the interview room, there's a certain amount of other preparation you must do. How exactly are you going to respond to the standard questions you are bound to be asked? You need to rehearse short and pithy responses to such common basic queries as 'Why do you want the job?', 'Why do you think you would be good at it?' and 'Why are you leaving your present job?' A fuller list of the standard questions that are always asked at interviews follows below. Careers are made or broken on the back of a few well-thought-out or ill-chosen words. While, in political life, sound-bites are commonly derided, having some of your own, provided they are not too glib, can make your day.

Normally people try to get by with adequate interpersonal skills in everyday life, but these are seldom enough to make a serious impact during an often tense and sometimes very brief and superficial job or promotion interview. You are almost certainly in competition with several other candidates. No matter how good your skills and aptitudes are, they are worthless unless you can communicate them effectively and immediately to others *within the time allowed*. You have, without being pushy, going over the top or being impertinent, to find a way to stand out in the crowd. You need to put across a few key points about yourself and cut out any needless or boring information. You cannot afford to interview badly – life is too competitive. There is nothing to beat live training in interview skills and watching and learning from the experience of friends and colleagues. Rehearse with them what you are going to say. Swap roles, ask yourself how you would advise *them* to improve, then draw the necessary lessons for yourself.

Now for a really significant fact in most selection processes. Believe it or not, it is all too common for an interviewer, doing a trawl for the right candidate for a job, merely to glance through a CV (which in my experience is all the attention that most CVs get), and from that to make certain rapid pre-judgements about whether or not you are even worth putting on a shortlist. After that, CVs are taken for granted; they are there to be referred to if some specific question arises. As you climb up the managerial or authority pyramid, they become less and less useful and are never going to get you a job on their own. Looking at it from the point of view of the interviewer or potential employer, when you are up for a serious job, many of the background details like the number of O-levels you once obtained, or what degree you have, tend to have little or no relevance, except as stimuli for questions such as 'I see you once did so and so', where the interviewer is not interested in your answer so much as how you answer. When selector comes face to face with candidate, the Primacy Effect outweighs such facts many times over.

Making your Mark

Just as we all do in life all the time, interviewers will filter out, from the huge amount of detailed evidence available, a very few basic items about you on which to base their final decision. You have very little time to make such people want to employ you. You need, for example, to dress to match the occasion. No matter how good your qualifications, if you come clothed like a down-and-out, looking shop-soiled with a badly ironed skirt or shirt, few are going to select you. Look back at all the points on dress, hairstyle, posture and paralanguage that we discussed in Chapter 3: such details will make or break you now. This is because as a general rule our attention is drawn towards stimuli that are attractive rather than offensive, bright rather than dull, confident rather than quiet, strong rather than weak, standing out rather than merged with their surroundings. How you present yourself has to signal a style to mark you out with those whom you intend to impress. I am not advocating that you rush out and buy a canary yellow suit and talk like a carpet salesman on speed, but you have to muster your attributes to best advantage to match your particular audience. How you enter that room, greet people, shake hands, and exude a certain amount of confidence can cause you to win or lose. At the very beginning of this book I said that I had seen many an interview lost in the few seconds between the candidate entering the room and sitting down at the table. If you think all interviewers are wise, objective, all-seeing, and will give you a huge amount of in-depth attention, you are seriously wrong. They are as fallible and biased as the rest of us.

I have seen interviews lost by such inconsequential features as the candidate slouching, mumbling, wearing an absurdly inappropriate tie, or, as a woman, by having a seriously plunging neckline, too short a skirt, or wearing too much costume jewellery. I have actually seen and heard top-level directors of major international plcs, who should have been choosing someone on the basis of their accountancy or legal skills, marking people down on the basis that 'If he couldn't even be bothered to sit up' or 'If she shows such a lack of judgement coming in dressed like a cheap tart ... what'll he/she be like if we gave them the job?' Gender and age perceptions and attitudes, both favourable and unfavourable, affect the coolest judgements of those who are

The Primacy Effect starts here

trying to make a selection. It may be wrong, it may be politically incorrect, it may lead to idiotic decisions over appointing or not appointing someone, but these are the facts of everyday selection life.

Whether or not some psychologists are right in claiming that deep down people are always seduced into appointing neo-clones, you will certainly discriminate in favour of a person who has characteristics acceptable or attractive to you. You may think you are icily immune from bias, but if you see in someone else a trait that is shared by you, or if you see characteristics or looks or habits or background that are common to people you like, then the stranger sitting in front of you will, as we saw in the earlier discussion about the Halo Effect, be imbued with other favourable characteristics which you assume they have, even though there is not a shred of evidence for such a belief.

Preparing the Ground

There is not a great deal you can do about certain preset, predetermined prejudices. If those who are going to be interviewing you don't like black skins or red hair or people in glasses, and you happen to have such defining attributes, then too bad – you are probably better off not working for them in any case. But there are a lot of areas where you can improve. Among things to think about are:

- Who is to interview you: an individual or a panel? What can you find out about them, their interests and likely prejudices?
- What exactly is the job/position? Research it and the company organization as much as you can.
- What are they looking for in terms of skills and experience?
- What good qualities about you do you want them to notice?
- How can you avoid revealing your less good qualities – the flipside factor?
- What should you wear for best effect? Always avoid extremes of dress.
- Ask yourself: How am I going to appeal? Why should they listen to me? Why should they want me?
- Remember the Fifteen-Second Rule: the Primacy Effect.
- Don't talk too much, but get the basic message about yourself, your Unique Selling Point, across.
- Rehearse and rehearse your answers to all the standard questions (see the list below).
- Work out your key message. In most interviews you will only have time to put across a maximum of three points.
- Prepare yourself for the unexpected question: you have to be ready with a powerful *response* rather than a precise answer.

Your message and your manner are inextricably linked. Perform well and you and your qualities shine through. You must, above all, prepare to go into any interview with a body language and paralanguage that lives up to and reinforces your words. Creating the right balance of assertiveness and impact that projects your personal competence, without overstating your case, wins the day.

A behavioural checklist should include the following:

- Enter the room confidently. Try a pleasant smile.
- Shake hands firmly. A weak damp handshake is always read as the mark of a weak person.
- Sit up and look alert.

- Look at who is asking the questions. Too much eye movement can make you look shifty. Listen actively.
- Watch your hand movements. Avoid gestures that distract attention or suggest excessive nervousness.
- Speak clearly.
- Watch your time: it's short.
- Be positive but not pushy.
- Don't ramble. Keep it tight.
- You know more about what you are going to say than they do. Most interviews end with them asking you whether you have any more questions or points you would like to raise? Pause and think.
- Make sure that *before you leave the room* you have said everything *you* wanted to say.

The Twenty Key Questions

With the help of successive years of my MBA students at Strathclyde Graduate Business School, I have drawn up the following list of twenty questions that come up again and again and again in job interviews. Try as we might, we seldom manage to add to them, though they are often expressed in very different ways. In various guises, in addition to any purely technical or factual questions about you and the vacancy, of course, they are asked whatever the level of the job to be filled. It is only sensible to work out ready answers to each and all of them.

1. What are your strengths and weaknesses?
2. Why do you want this job?
3. Why do you want to work for this company/organization?
4. How much does the money (remuneration package) matter?
5. What type of management do you like to work under: to be left to your own devices or be strongly directed?
6. What type of manager are *you*?
7. Are you a team player or a solo performer?
8. What were you doing previously?
9. Why did you leave your last job?
10. Are you willing to work away from home?

11. What motivates you, and why?
12. What experience do you have of budgets and keeping to them?
13. Can you manage teams of people?
14. What can you do for us that others can't?
15. From what you know of the firm or organization, what changes would you like to bring about?
16. Where do you see yourself in 3/5 years' time?
17. What would you like to be remembered for in your last job?
18. What do you do in your spare time?
19. What family or background issues are there that should be brought to our attention?
20. What questions do you have for us / What do you want to know about us?

One last, positive, thought: if they like you enough, if they want to employ or upgrade you, even though you have certain negative aspects in your personal impact package, they will put the latter to one side. There is always hope!

Getting Your CV Right

Written communication is not a subject generally covered by this book, but once you've polished up your Primacy Effect, and despite what I said at the beginning of the chapter about the minor importance of the CV, what you do not want is to spoil it all by sending out the wrong signals in yours. Otherwise, networking apart, you are not even going to get to first base.

A CV cannot and should not try to say everything about you. It is only another tool, an introduction to you, so my advice, based on the experience of wading and sifting through foot-high piles of them many, many times in the past – and discarding most of them out of hand – is to note the following with care.

- Keep it to a maximum of two A4 pages, normal print size, and don't try to pack too much on to the page. Avoid the 'how many words can I get on these two pages' approach.

- An equally concise summary paragraph should go at the top of your CV itself, listing your key strengths.
- Some employers may say they want a handwritten covering letter in order, presumably, to make some judgement of your graphology. In this day and age, sadly, the impression is likely to be scruffy and unprofessional, so don't, unless you have to.
- It goes without saying that CVs should be well and clearly set out. Don't try to stand out by using coloured paper or too many design gimmicks, unless you are very clever. Mostly it just looks naff. Last-minute manuscript corrections look sloppy and uncaring.
- Don't write a book. I had one recently that must have been close on five thousand words long, bound in glossy covers and complete with several colour photographs of the candidate. It was right over the top.
- Key points right up front, please. We don't have time to go through your life history in chronological order to get to the nuts. And give your latest history first.
- If you are such a success story in your present job, a brief reason for why you are wanting to move on can help explain your motivations.
- Needless to say, if your covering letter or the opening paragraph of your CV does not even begin to explain why you think your background and experience match the job specification as advertised, and why you have applied for this particular post, your application will look like one of a job lot and is likely to be discarded in consequence.

As the last candidate for the vacant position of Deputy Manager left the room, Bill yawned, stretched in his seat and turned towards Dr Mackenzie, who was sitting in a corner behind him. She had been a spectator at the interviews; he was keen to hear her reactions.

'I'm totally confused,' said Bill, looking down at his notes. 'There were only five of them on the shortlist, and I can hardly remember one from the other already.'

'That's as usual,' said Ruth Mackenzie. 'Which is why, to get anywhere as a candidate, you have to have something that stands out. But in the right way of course. You remember the girl in the white blouse, I suspect.'

Bill smiled. 'For all the wrong reasons. I couldn't take my eyes off...'

'Quite so,' said Ruth. 'She thought she was putting up a good front. She was in her way, but I bet you didn't end up listening to much of what she was saying.'

'True,' said Bill. 'I'm not trying to be sexist but . . .'

'Another point well made, then. She should have stood out but not er . . . er . . . stood out.'

'If it were me, how would I set about standing out, then?' Bill asked. 'I seem to have done well enough in life without thinking about it very much.'

'Ah, but your career has almost always been with this one company. They've grown to know you, love you, hate you – the Recency Effect.'

'If I were changing companies . . .?' Bill speculated.

'All the usual things. Dress smartly, but not over the top. I like that new tie by the way. Come into the room confidently. Sit with poise and distinction. Look around as if you are in command of yourself if not of everyone else. Don't fiddle. Have your responses well rehearsed.'

'Tell me again: what d'you mean by responses?'

'If you're asked the sort of question which both gives you the opportunity to shine and to put forward the various points you want to make before the end of the interview, you've got to get start working hard. Say what you have to say. Nobody's going to come back at you and say, "But I didn't ask you that" – if you do it cleverly enough.'

'I get the point. But what if they don't ask me the cue question which allows me to tell them what a brilliant chap I am?'

'There's always a question that you can turn. It is rather like going into an examination – knowing a subject is useless unless you put it down on the paper. It's no use knowing what you want to say and what you want them to know about you unless you say it. It's as simple as that.'

Bill stood up and stretched again. 'That guy with the pink shirt, the flowery tie and the greying hair – I can't remember his name now but he stood out on the image front. Wrongly. He also threw the whole thing. He thought he was communicating, but he muttered and mumbled so much. I could hardly hear what he was saying.' Bill paused. 'He had a good CV though.'

'How much is that CV going to matter, when the poor chap couldn't come across better than he did?' said Ruth Mackenzie.

'He was lost from when he first came in. He looked so nervous, so dishevelled, I almost asked him to go out and come back in again, once he had pulled himself together. Could he have had a hangover? He didn't have any understanding of what we wanted, what he wanted, or what we were offering.'

'You've learned so fast, Bill, you're about to do me out of a job.' Ruth Mackenzie picked up her papers, swept them into her briefcase, stood up, smiled and left the room.

When she had gone, Bill went quietly over to a mirror, straightened his tie, combed his hair, brushed his shoulders, straightened up, practised one of his charming smiles at his reflection in the glass, threw his shoulders back, and followed her out of the room.

INTERVIEW SKILLS: CASE STUDY NO. 1

PERSONAL AND CONFIDENTIAL
REPORT FROM A & B EXECUTIVE SEARCH TO GROUP CHAIRMAN AND CEO

JOB TITLE

Managing Director, International Design Company

JOB SPECIFICATION

Apart from outstanding technical, design and managerial skills, the successful candidate will have to report to the Main Board on a wide range of strategic and operational matters and oversee marketing across a wide global customer base. He or she will have to have excellent communications skills in dealing with a staff of 200 and agents in over 50 countries.

REPORT ON SHORTLIST

Out of a list of around a dozen serious candidates we have produced the following shortlist of three. In each case, the interviewee has, on paper, an excellent track record and the required qualifications and experience for the post. Their CVs and employment histories are all broadly similar and in our view each would, in consequence, fill the job very satisfactorily. Again, each candidate's references are well balanced and no one of them had a head start prior to extensive interviews by us.

INTERVIEW REPORTS

Following is a brief assessment of each candidate:

CANDIDATE A

As his background experience and CV suggest, he is a top-flight candidate. He dresses and presents himself well and has a bright and lively personality. If anything, he showed that he was rather too full of himself, though it may well be that, in interview, he was somewhat nervous and was trying too hard. He is certainly a skilled communicator and is never short of words. He would, we think, inspire his staff very well, though his enthusiasms might from time to time get the better of him. A further plus point is that we judge he would not always try to force his own views on people, but be willing to take in suggestions from his creative team. He would certainly brand the Design Company very well to customers and clients given his high-profile style and drive. He was full of very good ideas. In sum, an excellent candidate though perhaps needing a bit of a steer or brake from time to time.

CANDIDATE B

He is a quieter candidate, much more soberly dressed and presented. He comes across as someone who is a bit over-serious but also very professional and efficient. We had initial doubts about his suitability for this particular position where a certain flair and style is necessary, but when he eventually relaxed, he showed a great deal more warmth and sparkle, an important example of nearly having been let down by the first impressions he gave us. He has a good sense of humour. Our recommendation is that while he might take longer to settle into the position and would not force himself on the management style at first, and doubtless would not hit clients quite so hard when he came to pitch to them, he would prove a resolute and dependable hand on the tiller in the long run.

CANDIDATE C

She is a very likeable and experienced woman in her mid-forties with outstanding background and experience. She is divorced. She is good-looking and well turned out without being too glamorous, and displays a steady quality about her which tends to confirm, as her references state, that she would make an excellent and popular Manager Director. Given the nature of the work, we can see no downside in appointing a woman to this post, indeed quite the reverse. She appears to get on well with staff of both sexes and, in terms of the image of the company, we can see certain distinct advantages in appointing her, if this is the Board's final choice.

OUTCOME

Each short-listed candidate was interviewed twice more by different members of the Board of Directors of the Group.

Candidate A ruled himself out early on. He was bright and amusing, but proved too pushy and full of himself to convince the interview panels that he was consistent enough to be able to manage a happy team.

Candidate C ruled herself out at the last fence because initial impressions proved deceptive. In negotiating her possible terms of employment she increasingly showed herself to be picky and pedantic, then demanding, even aggressive. This brought out elements of a latent style which convinced both male and female Board members that in the long run she might prove more trouble than she was worth.

While *Candidate B* on first sight did not seem an inspired choice, the Board eventually shared the Executive Search Company's view that his depth and warmth of personality would make him an excellent appointee.

INTERVIEW SKILLS: CASE STUDY NO. 2

CONFIDENTIAL
P & A SECRETARIAL RECRUITMENT LTD

JOB TITLE

Personal Assistant to the Chairman, Transnational plc

JOB SPECIFICATION

The candidate will almost certainly be female, bright, efficient and outward-looking, and be able to manage the Chairman's busy life, correspondence and schedules. There are two other more junior secretaries in the office whose work the candidate will have to oversee. This position will suit a highly motivated and experienced person who is also capable of being the in-house eyes and ears of her employer, ensuring that both he and his senior team are always fully and relevantly briefed.

REPORT ON SHORTLIST

Out of a very good field, no males figured. We have narrowed the list down to a shortlist of four, all with rather different backgrounds and experience, but in every case someone who we feel would fill this challenging job more than adequately.

INTERVIEW REPORTS

Following is a brief assessment of each candidate:

CANDIDATE A

A mature 45-year-old with a great deal of experience of working for Board level employers. Tough, old-school and hyper-efficient but with a wry sense of humour, she would fill the job admirably.

CANDIDATE B

A 38-year-old divorcee, who has recently come back to work after bringing up a family. She has all the necessary computer and word-processing skills, is charming and attractive, and claims that her residual domestic responsibilities will not interfere with what is normally a very heavy workload.

CANDIDATE C

This candidate is very bright, of West Indian origin, with all the necessary skills and an attractive, outgoing and lively personality. She is in her mid-thirties, divorced with no children.

CANDIDATE D

Much younger than the other three candidates, she is a 28-year-old graduate with much less experience of PA work than the others. She is, however, both highly skilled and self-motivated and would make an excellent and stimulating head of the Chairman's office.

OUTCOME

The Human Resources Director saw each candidate, as did the Chairman himself. After further discussion, they came to the following decisions:

Candidate D was ruled out because, despite a very lively personality, she did not come across as well enough turned out or formally enough spoken to handle the top-level visitors and callers she would meet on a daily basis. Her dress sense was felt not to be in keeping with company style, where the Chairman's PA would be expected to set an example. Her Liverpool accent was just too pronounced for the largely South-East of England clientele she would be dealing with. Her lack of experience also counted heavily against her, but most important of all, her own personal ambitions, as she expressed them herself, suggested that she might get bored with the routine chores which comprise much of the daily workload.

Candidate C also quickly ruled herself out. She is a very lively personality but her flamboyant appearance (which has nothing to do with her ethnic background) suggested to the Chairman that she might be too much of a good thing. He always likes to keep his door open and her loud voice and louder laugh, while infectious, would, he felt, be a disturbing factor in his outer office. His declared preference is for someone much more methodical, even if a bit conventional.

Candidate B was ruled out for the same reason. She did, after questioning, also admit that, deep down, she was personally concerned, because of her domestic arrangements, about the late hours she might from time to time be required to work.

Candidate A has been offered and has accepted the position.

CHAPTER 6

Private Conversation
and Public Speaking

Talking and eloquence are not the same: to speak and to speak well are two things.

Ben Jonson

I've been asked to speak to you. You've been asked to listen to me. If you finish before me...

Michael Sinclair

Always be shorter than anybody dared to hope.
Lord Reading

Be sincere, be brief, be seated.
Franklin D. Roosevelt

The object of oratory is not truth, but persuasion.
Thomas Babington Macaulay

One interlocutor or a sea of faces. You begin to speak. Can you make your points clearly and well or will you seize up and your mind go blank? Great negotiators, like great orators, come but seldom into this world, yet effective public speakers can be made. Public speaking is a learnable art, best done with the help of a skilled teacher who will show you how to project your voice with variety and confidence.

Every day we see people in our lives or on our television screens making a mess of things by coming across badly. Not everyone needs to become a charismatic performer or lecturer or a brilliant after-dinner speaker. If you at least enunciate clearly, with definition and conviction in everyday conversation as well, your audience, whether of one or a hundred, will listen to you. Here is some practical advice on how you can improve.

It was Mike Deaver, President Reagan's pre-eminent spin-doctor, who introduced me to the word *mediagenic* – used to describe something contrived to look highly appealing to the news media. As he said about Reagan's first trip to China, it was a long way to take a President to get him photographed standing on a Wall, but in terms of personal image and international recognition, it worked. The world saw, it listened and it was impressed.

In ordinary life, some people have a natural gift of making other people listen. Their speech comes out relaxed, witty, spontaneous, thoughtful. Others open their mouths and are an immediate switch-off, like the speaker who asked his audience if everyone could hear him, to which the cynical heckle came back: 'I can, but I'll gladly swap with someone who can't.' In addressing other people, you can generally gauge your personal impact credit-rating by a careful reading of the signs of how others read you. They listen intently, they look interested or bored or hostile. In the following attempt to ensure that none of your words fall on deaf ears, there may appear to be some gimmicks included, but in essence public speaking, like good conversation, is not a gimmicky subject. You only have to remind yourself, once again, how many causes have been lost, not because of the substance or the subject-matter, but because of bad presentation and bad impacting, and to identify what it was that destroyed the credibility which the subject deserved. I have listened to many bad speakers in my time and few get away with it, though one, the late President of Romania, Nicolae Ceaucescu, who would drone on for four or five hours to the Central Committee of the Communist Party, did get listened to: his bored audience knew what would happen to them if they did not.

Any speaker's words are subjected to the immediate test of the audience's reaction to them. Any audience will compare you with the best that has gone before you and mark you up or down accordingly. Before you open your mouth, therefore, you should always be sure that:

- You know your subject.
- You believe in your subject.
- You have practised your delivery.
- You know your audience and what its reaction to you and the subject is likely to be.

Rhetoric

Oratory, or rhetoric, is often referred to as a dying art, or at least one that has fallen well out of fashion. Before the advent of mass communication, it was something worthy of careful study. Books were written about it, teaching was given in it, and it was a skill of such major political and social significance that no person in public life could possibly succeed without it. It still should be so.

The skill of rhetoric, using language boldly and imaginatively in such a way as to persuade an audience, was first taught in Greece by the so-called Sophists. They used it in highly structured forms to argue claims in court cases and elsewhere, and any speech was always divided into various distinct parts, including the narrative, the argument, subsidiary remarks and the so-called peroration. It was Aristotle, however, who insisted that rhetoric was an art form because if any speaker was particularly persuasive, it was always possible to define why he or she had succeeded in being so. He went on to argue that while playing on the emotions of an audience was all very well, the

He gets listened to because of who he is. Why should people listen to you?

true aim of real rhetoric was to prove a point by the use of logic.

Later masters of rhetoric said that logic alone was not enough; to carry an audience one always had to appeal to the emotions and passions of those who were listening. Speakers could be successful if they used the correct rhetorical devices. It was, consequently, a skill that could be widely abused. History has indeed turned up many public figures with a dangerous ability to persuade audiences and to inflame base emotions without recourse to fact. One only has to think of Hitler, Mussolini and other great dictators.

Members of other rhetorical schools devoted huge amounts of time and study to making their art ever more sophisticated and convoluted, to impress the multitude with the cleverness and style of their delivery. From the Middle Ages to the late seventeenth century, any young university undergraduate had to study rhetoric, but in the eighteenth century it began to die away as a formal subject for study. Whatever name we give it today, the art of speaking clearly and persuasively is one that too many people fail to cultivate.

We have to look far to find people whom we would describe as having great rhetorical abilities in contemporary life. For years, MPs of all parties consistently voted for two men, one of the extreme right and one of the extreme left, Enoch Powell and Tony Benn, as being among the best speakers and debaters in the House of Commons. Both spoke with a precision and clarity and an absence of dependence on notes that few others could emulate. There are some very cogent political speakers around, notably Donald Dewar and Malcolm Rifkind, who are precise in argument and diction as befits their Scottish legal backgrounds. The range and structure of their vocabulary makes what they say sound almost like written English, since each sub-paragraph is precise in its grammatical form and each sentence has a clear beginning, middle and end.

Otherwise the recent tendency in public life, but especially across the dispatch boxes in the House of Commons, is towards sneers, heckling, the cheap phrase and the quick sound-bite. Nobody has time for oratory. Much to our surprise, however, from across the Atlantic, even from President Clinton, we sometimes get good impassioned speeches, impressively delivered. There is greatness in some of the words of recent American Presidents. Their speech-writers are an accomplished bunch.

Sadly, in Britain, great words, great feelings, if expressed at all, are condemned as banal. In any case, most great speeches retain little of their flavour when consigned to the printed page; without a commentary, even most of Hansard's immaculate parliamentary reporting fails to come alive. One has to have been present to understand the tone and resonance of most occasions. By contrast, some of President Clinton's words, read afterwards, still impart a glow. Here the sentences have been carefully modulated and the messages tightly crafted. What sometimes lets the President down is his body language; adding to the negatives of his reputation, he seems to smirk, which can be irritating to a European audience. He looks rather too pleased with himself, but as he has grown into office, he has gained the transitory gravitas of a distinguished international statesman. We in Britain have to go back to the speeches of Macmillan and Churchill, or even to the nineteenth-century figures such as Gladstone who would address audiences of up to 20,000, to get a sense of real rhetoric.

What the American President or his advisers realize is that making a speech is a very serious matter. If you make a bad twenty-minute speech to a hundred people, that is not just twenty minutes of your time, but a total of over two or three days of other people's lives wasted. Even if you yourself seldom have to stand up and make a big set-piece speech, in most senior positions you will daily be required to speak aloud at Board meetings, to groups of friends or colleagues, or make a sales pitch to half a dozen potential clients around a table. In each case, exactly the same techniques are required.

As actors rehearse their parts, so your public speaking skills can be radically improved by constant practice. If you work as hard at your delivery as you do on your text, improving your mannerisms and your voice projection, your overall confidence will grow. Only three things matter: how you look, how you say what you have to say, and what you say. Of the three, and there will still be doubters on this, the last matters least. Your approach should start, as before, with looking hard at how you appear, even if it is only using a mirror to proper advantage. People always believe more of what they see than of what they hear. Look closely at yourself. Do you *look* believable?

No one can wave a wand and make you into a great speaker, but good tuition can make you passably effective, just as fumbling, inarticulate shambles of an interviewee *can* be taught to put a case across without too many problems. Huge and rapid improvements can be made even after a single day's training. You *can* learn to speak confidently. You *can* conquer nerves. Both come with the assurance that practice brings.

Your Voice

A practical first step again is to become fully conversant with the sound of your own voice. Tape yourself just reading aloud from a book or article, and play the result back. Listen carefully. Are you pleased or horrified at the sound? Is what you hear gentle or strident, hesitant or resonant, convincing or off-putting? What of your timing and pace? Do you sound interesting or boring? If you can take and trust their judgement, what do family, friends or close colleagues really think of your performance?

When you listen to your own voice on tape, remember that everyone reacts negatively or positively to voices that they find insipid, harsh or pleasing. If you listen to a lot of radio, you'll appreciate that a voice that suits a pop music station will hardly possess the authority required of a news-reader or a political commentator on BBC Radio 4. In day-to-day life, irrespective of what is being said, we react differently to voices that suggest power or weakness, that seek to persuade, that are querulous, kindly or bad-tempered. Women can have particular difficulties with their public voices and their paralanguage, a subject we will return to in more detail in a later chapter. Too often what they intend as 'authoritative' comes out sounding strident or screechy, while too soft a voice suggests weakness. For reasons which are not entirely clear, it is particularly difficult for a woman's voice to hold the attention of a mixed audience, for instance as an after-dinner speaker. The mix of gravitas and lightness that is required often appears to be difficult for women to master, though there are some very notable exceptions.

We touched on the question of accent earlier in the book, but, as always, acceptable pronunciation depends on the ear of the listener. In Britain, Received Standard English and Received Pronunciation, the particular pronunciation of British English which, to quote the dictionary definition, is generally regarded as being least regionally limited and the most socially acceptable, is undoubtedly a plus point if you are putting across a message to a national audience. It can, however, provoke mirth or derision from an audience in a Glasgow or Liverpool pub.

Any public utterance by you has, from the outset, to be handled like a public performance, with an in-built 'entertainment' factor. It may sound way over the top, but whether you are making a boardroom presentation, or giving a short impromptu talk, a lecture, or a major after-dinner speech, this is always true. You are on parade, to be praised or criticized for succinctness and wit and clarity of delivery more than for content. At the next office meeting or lecture you go to, look around carefully and you will see what I mean.

Audience and Location

Next, you need to identify precisely what kind of audience you are to address. Is it fairly heterogenous, or is it one made up of people with differing attitudes and expectations of you? Do they know each other? What are they expecting? Why should they listen to you? The one piece of good news is that *most* audiences are benign to start off with. You have to bring them with you, making them part of your performance.

The next step, particularly with big spenders or presentations, is to familiarize yourself with the territory in which you are going to have to perform. You need to case the joint, insisting on testing the acoustics and the microphone if there is one, since even in the best-regulated settings there can be feedback whine. All the most experienced speakers go through this check. If you do not do this and simply appear at the podium or in the briefing room at the last moment and begin by asking if people can hear you at the back, or indulge in a teach-in game with the audience over whether your audio visual aids can be seen and so on, you have prepared badly and are letting yourself down. W. H. Auden, starting a lecture in a large hall, gave the ultimate warning on all this: 'If there are any of you at the back who cannot hear me, please don't bother to raise your hands because I am also near-sighted.'

Here is a checklist of key points to consider:

- How big is the room? This is important in terms of the volume and speed at which you are going to have to deliver your message. The larger the room, the slower will be your pace.
- How near will people be to you? Are the front rows likely to be empty (a common experience), or will they be sitting so close to you that they can read your notes before you do? Can you rearrange their seating or yours, or your table or lectern to suit your preference?
- The microphone: does it work without adjustment? Is it at the right height? A microphone, like a lectern, can sometimes appear like a barrier, so try to do without one if you can.
- The height of the lectern, if there is one: will your notes stay on the gradient? Pre-position your notes on the lectern if you can be sure they will be left undisturbed until you get there.
- Is there water to hand? Even the most experienced speakers get dry mouths. Remove bulky objects and distractingly noisy small change from your pockets.
- What is the lighting like? Will it blind you? If they dim the lights when you stand up to speak, will you be able to read your notes? Where are you to sit prior to and after the speech? Will you have to stumble up and down in the dark?
- The audience: will it be lively or soporific? How big is it? Could it be hostile or even slightly inebriated, depending on the time of day? Are they there to be

informed, persuaded or entertained? What are their age and sex? Are they seated directly in front of you, or spread out through 180 degrees? The latter will require you to do a lot more looking to left and right to establish the necessary rapport with them.

- If you intend to use teleprompts, monitors or reflective glass cue screens, have you practised enough?
- Who are the other speakers? Are they likely to conflict or overlap with you, outshine you, or steal your jokes or your punchlines?
- Finally, what are you hoping to achieve? What effect do you want to have? *Do not enter the room until you are entirely clear about that.*

Coping with Nerves

The human brain starts working the moment you are born and never stops until you stand up to speak in public.

Sir George Jessel

Stage fright is very common. Even many highly successful actors are physically sick before the opening night. Apprehension can, however, get the adrenalin working and put you on a high, and people frequently feel much more nervous than they actually appear. Clients and students constantly ask me whether I noticed that their hands were shaking or that they nearly dried up, and my honest response is usually no. But I do not believe that anyone is entirely free of nerves before making a public speech. While no book can teach you how to beat nervousness, one way to start to do so is to try to identify the root cause of your problem. What exactly are you afraid of? Among the most common causes are:

- Fear of peer group mockery
- Fear of drying up/losing your place
- Lack of knowledge of the subject
- Fear of being boring
- Fear of losing your audience's attention
- Fear of generally making a fool of yourself

You're in Charge

Relaxation techniques cannot be taught from a book either, but the following are keys to help you assert your own personal mastery of any occasion.

- Arrive well in advance. Familiarize yourself totally with the location. *This is your turf.* Think: I am in charge here! Everyone else is a visitor.
- Keep remembering that you know more than anyone in the audience about what you want to say. Confidence comes most easily from a total mastery of your subject.
- Keep remembering that you are in control of the occasion.
- Pre-relax your body. One common method is to stretch, tense and relax your shoulders, then do the same with your arms, ending by flopping them to your sides. Gently continue to shake your arms to remove rigidity and tension, letting them go limp before you stand to speak. Avoid hyper-ventilating by practising deep, regular breathing rather than going for short, nervous breaths. *Feel yourself into that control.*
- When you stand up, speak slightly louder than you might otherwise do. Speak with authority. I have constantly found while teaching that the sound of a pupil's own voice, if loud, positive and assertive enough, actually builds up his or her confidence. In practice sessions, I get my most nervous clients to speak far, far louder than they need, almost shouting the words so that they can gradually assert their total control of the situation by hearing their own potential vocal strength.
- Never use alcohol to relax. You may think it helps. It does not.
- Speak as naturally as possible. Anyone who has had to listen to a lot of public speeches knows about the special 'speech voice' which many would-be orators adopt. They think it makes them sound more authoritative. It usually ends up being ponderous or contrived.
- Make sure your script, if you have one, is written in 'spoken' English. Too many people draft speeches in highly grammatical English which comes across as very stilted when delivered. Spoken English, by contrast, can be highly ungrammatical, using broken, unfinished sentences to add feeling and sincerity. Listen out for this in your own voice on tape. Do not attempt to disguise your accent unless it is so pronounced that it could interfere with the audience's understanding.

- If there is a lectern, hold on, lightly but firmly, to its sides. It stops handshake. Begin by focusing on one or two sympathetic figures in the audience if it helps reassure you.
- Keep your speech short.
- Keep it as light as possible, commensurate with the subject. Pomposity kills.

Speech Content

Never rise to speak till you have something to say; and when you have said it, cease.

John Witherspoon

Sheridan once said of some speech, in his acute, sarcastic way, that 'It contained a great deal both of what was new and what was true; but what was new was not true and what was true was not new.'

William Hazlitt

After the initial formalities, any speech must begin with an explanation of what you are going to say. Make your agenda clear from the outset. A speech must have a nub, a fulcrum, a heart, backed up with a few powerful illustrations and some memorable key phrases. Preachers get your attention by telling a parable, which leads on to the main message of the sermon. You can illustrate any argument in a similar way. Because all audiences, and not just religious congregations, are lazy and need reminding, inject a certain amount of repetition towards the end. Telling them what you have told them never comes amiss.

Know what is expected. So often I have seen a speaker turn up ill-briefed or ill-prepared and eventually leave a bored or disappointed audience behind. Be clear whether you are meant to be entertaining or advocating some cause, or is it to be a bit of both?

Never begin with *any apologies* for your content, your subject, your style or anything else. As someone once said, 'Why doesn't the person who stands up and says "I'm not a speech-maker" let it go at that instead of giving us a lengthy demonstration?'

There are a number of guidelines on which any good speech-writer tends to rely. These are:

- Put in a punchy opener to wake people up and grab their attention.
- Develop that main theme with a clear beginning, middle and end.
- Illustrate that theme with a human interest story.
- Personalize the message. Talk about things from your own and your audience's point of view. The use of 'I', 'you' and 'we' tends to bond audience and speaker.
- To repeat: remember the difference between words and sentences that are written for reading and those chosen for speaking aloud. The length of sentences is crucial: spoken sentences are best short and smart.
- Watch out for sensitive issues that can alarm, irritate or antagonize. If your jokes tend to be earthy, make sure that all your audience is of that ilk too. I have seen offended people walking out.
- In a speech, signposts are needed to help the listeners remember. 'I would like to make three points. First … etc.' Avoid complex parenthetical clauses.
- Avoid too many facts and figures. Details are difficult to remember. A speech is not a lecture.
- Don't be afraid of repetition. Find a punchy and telling conclusion. Get that off pat. A fluffed last sentence is a killer.

Abraham Lincoln always said that you should treat audiences as having an average age of nine. Incidentally, the Gettysburg Address only consisted of around two hundred words and took only two or three minutes to deliver.

With this in mind, to summarize: a speech has to be simple, it has to be pungent, and the sentences have to be crisp. Anything long and rambling ought to be broken up. When you have written it, read it out loud to make sure that the cadences and the structure flow properly. Audiences have a very short memory span, so keep the argument simple. Repeat to remind and always summarize at the end.

Full Text or Notes?

If you want me to talk for ten minutes, I'll come next week. If you want me to talk for an hour, I'll come tonight.

Woodrow Wilson

Professionals disagree over whether you should work from a full text or notes. Some of the best speeches have neither. My advice is that, for major occasions, unless or until you are very skilled at it, you should prepare a full text to fall back on. Again I stress that it should be a text that is written for speaking, and not for reading. For speaking, we do not need perfect prose, nor complete sentences, nor exact subordinate clauses. We can allow ourselves great simplicity and repetition with the spoken word, because even an alert audience needs more time to assimilate facts that they hear than ones that they read. It should be a text that is not too complex, that is not merely a list of key issues or points. Your speaking style can be varied and fragmented and yet successful; it can lack perfect smoothness yet deliver a punch; it can be memorable without being too polished and grammatical. You can refer to your text, but if possible try to avoid being seen to read from it. It is really only necessary to read aloud where it is a detailed factual lecture or where the precise words need to be very strictly adhered to.

Once you have written out the full text, there are various methods of progressing thereafter. I tend to summarize my main points on eight-by-five-inch cue or index cards (not on sheets of paper, which, if you are nervous, will flutter and exaggerate any hand shake), each of which contains one major point or key phrase, such as the final sentence of all. Points should, if possible, not run over from one card to another. An alternative is to underline, or highlight with a yellow marker, key words or phrases on the full text itself, which will give you a steer without tempting you to read from the text.

Your Delivery

There are a number of things to remember about your actual delivery. Some are repetitions of things said above, because they are worth repeating.

- Create the right impact as you walk to the lectern or stand up to speak. You know what you want to say. Stand up there with authority. Look around slowly.

Pause. Wait until all superfluous noise, such as the clatter of waiters clearing away dishes or serving coffee, is at a minimum.

- Eye-swing from left to right round your audience. Pick out one or two fairly friendly faces and keep returning to them. It helps you personalize your delivery and develops trust on both sides.
- Your formal opening should be delivered slowly to gain attention. 'Mr Chairman, Ladies and Gentlemen' etc. Wait for silence to fall.
- You are there to make them like you. You have to try to entertain in order to convince, winning audience as well as argument.
- Your expression matters. Try, if not to smile, at least to keep a pleasant expression.
- It is nonsense to think you can over-rehearse. The more practising you do, with friends or with a video camera, the better.
- Speak rather too loudly than the reverse. Speak so that the back row can hear clearly.
- Personalize your text. Get someone with experience to run through your text with you and listen to you.
- Keep it short. Almost no speech should be longer than ten minutes, particularly after dinner.
- Be careful not to slip into reading from your prepared text half-way through. This is a *very* common fault.
- Do not go too fast. Avoid gabbling or swallowing words, or running phrases into each other. The larger the audience or room, the slower you have to speak.
- Pauses can be the most dramatic thing in your whole performance. They can catch the attention of the audience, especially if they are slightly too long, but don't make them so long that people think you have dried up or lost your place.
- Speak, look down and consult your notes, look up, then speak again. i.e. you should speak only when you are looking at your audience, not when your eyes are staring down at your text or notes.
- Unless you are a natural, do not try to memorize the whole thing. It can so easily let you down.
- Do not ad lib unless you are really experienced.

What you do with your hands is a subject in itself. I tend to hold lightly on to a lectern if there is one, until I get the feel of my speech, my confidence, and my audience. Having reached that point, I try using simple, confident gestures with one hand and arm to emphasize my words. Never put your hands in your trouser pockets: it looks too laidback, if not slovenly; and folding your arms looks oddly defensive, while if you have them clasped behind your back it can give you too military a flavour. The old-fashioned hooking of the thumbs into the arms of a waistcoat tends to look odd nowadays, though some characterful speakers still get away with it.

Body Language at the Podium

Never make a gesture from the elbow – that's a very weak gesture ... If you make it at all it must come from the shoulder.

Harold Macmillan

Here's another variety of checklist:

- Smarten up. Men, adjust your tie before going on stage.
- Make a 'stage' entry.
- Stand upright but easily balanced. Try not to sway or rock.
- Don't fiddle. Avoid distractions such as jangling money in your pockets, playing with your hair, your collar or your spectacles.
- Watch your hands. Turn fiddles into gestures, using your notes or your spectacles, if you have them, for emphasis, raising them in your hand to make a point. A symbolic clubbing movement, with the arm raised, can produce splendid emphasis.
- Don't give the impression that you're hiding or sheltering behind the lectern. Men, if standing with no lectern between them and the audience, should avoid protectively clasping their hands in front of their flies. It can cause mirth.
- Handle your notes precisely or discreetly. Don't shuffle them.
- After your final sentence, pause, look round and leave the stage with dignity. Don't run as if you want to hide, even if you do.

The Uses and Misuses of Humour

Once you get people laughing, they're listening and you can tell them almost anything.

Herbert Gardner

With respect to Mr Gardner, whoever he was, unless you are the one in a hundred who is naturally funny, take great care. Humour has many, many pitfalls. Again there are a few simple rules:

- Don't if you can't. If you are bad at telling jokes, don't try.
- If you are likely to throw or mistime the punchline, forget it.
- Avoid long stories or anecdotes unless you are a good story-teller.
- Stick to quick, apt, one-liners, but rehearse them well.
- Never announce a joke in advance, and never apologize for one either.
- Make sure it is original. Old jokes kill. People will not remember if you repeat the serious parts of your speech, but they will never forgive you if you've told them the same joke before.
- Don't be smutty unless you really know your audience. Ask yourself: Is it relevant? Is it acceptable? Always opt for caution.

Those Few Informal Words

It takes more than three weeks to prepare a good impromptu speech.

Mark Twain

If you are required to make a few casual remarks, this requires just as much thinking about as any major speech. You can, with a few words, have an effect with some quick and light turn of phrase that might not stand up to scrutiny in front of a large and hungry audience. But a farewell speech for someone leaving the office, a brief vote of thanks, a few words at a friendly dinner party, should be well prepared in advance even though you intend to be on your feet for less than a minute. Short means pithy and to the point. You have no time to be eloquent. Then stop.

Autocues

If you need them, well, you need them. Some autocues are very sophisticated, but they will, unless you handle them well, quickly reveal that you are merely reading your lines. A real speech has hesitations and spontaneity. Sir Robin Day has argued that only Ronald Reagan could use one well, but then he was a professional actor. To quote Day (and his autobiography is well worth reading on this and on many other 'personal impact' subjects): 'For someone trying to persuade, or amuse, or inspire their audience, as a politician or public figure may wish to do, then the use of the autocue is liable to kill personality, sincerity and spontaneity ... I have never seen or heard a rip-roaring, passionate, witty or inspiring platform speech delivered from autocue.'

Audio-visual Aids

I make no attempt here to cover what is a well-discussed subject, beyond saying that a speech or a lecture should never debase itself by becoming an adjunct to, or the mere narration of, a slide show. As I write, I am still recovering from a night where the speaker at an awards ceremony merely read out the text of each slide he screened. We read them quicker than he could. He spoke for half an hour. Boredom set in after two minutes. By all means project images that can do a job more effectively than words, such as graphs or pie charts. Otherwise, my advice is – bin them. A visual aid, slide or whatever, should be that and that alone, a back-up to the real message. The same goes for blackboards, whiteboards, flip charts and film. If you *are* going to use them, get them in the right order, the right way up. There is no excuse for a sloppy audio-visual presentation.

Question and Answer Sessions

Let your speech be always with grace, seasoned with salt, that ye may know how ye ought to answer every man.

The Bible: Colossians

There are no hard and fast rules about how to deal with the question and answer sessions which sometimes follow a speech. It is, however, a good idea for the Chairman of the session, or you yourself, to repeat the question. It helps the audience, particularly if the questioner was difficult to hear in a large room or hall, and it also gives you time to think. Even the silliest questions should be treated with great patience and courtesy. The audience may laugh at a naïve questioner: you should not, ever.

Hostile Audiences

Most audiences are inclined to be kind at least at the beginning of the speech. You will never get reverence, but providing you follow the rules and do not insult or bore people, you will go a long way before you start being heckled. It may be, of course, that you are already known for some extreme view, or that the audience consists of 500 angry mill workers whom you are about to sack, in which case you may have an uphill struggle.

Here the five basic rules are:

1. If you can't cope, don't try.
2. Never lose your temper. React with equanimity even when provoked.
3. Try to get the majority on your side.
4. Don't let the occasion degenerate into a slanging match.
5. Volunteer to discuss issues privately with persistent hecklers later.

The Ending of Your Speech

Follow the advice I was given when singing in supper clubs. 'Get off while you're ahead; always leave them wanting more.'

Dorothy Sarnoff

A speech is a love affair. Any fool can start it, but to end it requires considerable skill.

Lord Mancroft

There are two little words which will catch the attention of even the most apathetic audience. These are: 'In conclusion ...' Conclusions are an important part of every speech. They are especially welcome when they come close to the beginning. Some speakers, however, seem to get a second wind from then on. Make sure that what follows this is very brief indeed. Memorize that final sentence and make it upbeat and punchy. Fluffing the last line can kill the lot.

'So . . . full text or notes?' asked Bill.

'It all comes with practice,' Ruth Mackenzie responded. 'When you stand up to speak, you ought to know more about your subject than the audience does, so you shouldn't need a text. Some of the greatest speeches were points jotted down on the back of an envelope, to help the speaker keep to a reasonably disciplined agenda. It sounds like a truism but a speech spoken from the heart is worth a thousand pages of copy. People will forgive you any number of 'ums' and 'ers' and repetitions if it is truly spontaneous. What they will never forgive you for is a long drone, particularly late at night. Appeal to their emotions . . .'

'Have them reaching for a handkerchief?' Bill grinned.

'I'm not joking. If you can make them laugh or listen in stunned silence to some story, that's the way to get their attention. Humanizing your message with a clever anecdote always pays dividends.'

'I've only heard a handful of great speeches in my life, and read fewer.'

'That's the trouble with speeches. Some of the best never had a text. You had to be there to appreciate them. Remember that speech by Geoffrey Howe, when he finally put the boot into Margaret Thatcher? The text itself doesn't look up to much. You had to be sitting in the House of Commons to realize the sheer venom behind that piece of history in the making.'

'Hand movements?'

'The only way to see how good your body language is is to watch yourself on a video recording with the sound turned down. Write down your faults and run through it again. Whatever you do, however, make strong gestures, not limp-wristed affairs. By the way, what was that last good speech you heard all about?'

'God, he was funny! Never laughed so much. Real theatre,' said Bill.

'The subject?'

'Can't for the life of me remember.'

'You've made the point for me once again, Bill. Thanks very much.'

MS CONSULTANTS
TRAINING PROGRAMME NO. 2

CANDIDATE: NEW CHAIRMAN OF PRIVATIZED WATER COMPANY

CONFIDENTIAL BACKGROUND REPORT

Following the much publicized and ridiculed resignation of the water company's previous Chairman, MS Consultants has been asked to train the new Chairman prior to his first exposure to what is liable to be a highly critical public and news media. Though efficient, the previous Chairman left under a cloud despite his having brought about certain notable company successes, solely because of his public image and his disastrous handling of the media. The Company's head of Public Affairs left last year, claiming that his advice was always ignored. His successor wisely realizes that while he can do a lot of the grassroots PR, the public tends to personify the water company, in that it has to be the top man who argues the case well, or takes the fall-out.

REPORT

The Chairman is very willing but not a natural extrovert. He has come up through the ranks of the industry and, while very popular with those who know him, does not come across particularly well in front of an external audience. He tries very hard, but on the charisma scale he is never going to rate very highly. He is, however, a patently sincere and genuine man who is instantly likeable, and while he will never make a great orator, we will try to encourage him to speak as much as he can without notes, since his eye contact is good and he tends to smile agreeably at those to whom he is speaking.

The video playback system has proved invaluable to this candidate. His body language is good, and now that we have succeeded in getting him to speak more slowly, he already sounds much more authoritative. We have persuaded his staff to cut back on the amount of facts and figures they put into his speech drafts. He should be the broad-brush leader, concentrating on speaking at a human level. His Cornish accent, whilst quite pronounced, comes across warmly and well and, given the industry he is in, is an added plus point in his delivery style.

RESULTS

The Chairman has made modest but respectable improvements. Freed from repeating a long litany of facts and figures, and having slowed his delivery, he now appears as a trustworthy spokesman for the Company, with the welfare of his customers obviously of genuine concern to him. He is continuing to practise his interview skills and, without having to remember all the figures, is increasingly good at putting across the basic arguments that the public wants to hear.

CHAPTER 7

Negotiating, Networking
and Running Meetings

There are some people who leave impressions not
so lasting as the imprint of an oar upon the water.
Kate Chopin

If you wish in this world to advance
Your merits you're bound to enhance;
You must stir it and stump it,
And blow your own trumpet,
Or, trust me, you haven't a chance.
W.S. Gilbert, Ruddigore

If your lips would keep from slips,
Five things observe with care;
To whom you speak, of whom you speak,
And how, and when, and where.
W.E. Norris

You may be the best prepared, the most highly qualified and professional member of a team, but unless you have a grasp of tactics and timing in negotiating in any business or social relationship, you will fail. Persuading, pitching, marshalling the key argument in the best way to the right people: these are all essential skills which too many people think they have and too few do. Great cases and causes are lost, not because the ideas or the strategies are bad, but because of bad timing and bad presentation.

According to *The Times*, just before the last General Election, the then British Prime Minister, John Major, had a Road to Damascus conversion. He had decided that in future he would 'lead from the front, abandoning his past collegiate style and going for a tougher approach, issuing edicts and demanding results'. 'He has found a new authority,' informed sources went on to say. Whatever the truth, it did him little good, since public perceptions about the reputation of political figures cannot be changed so late in the day. As when altering a supertanker's course, you have to start turning the wheel a very long time in advance. One of the most curious examples of how such reputations are made and stick, while the maker seems not to have left, to quote American commentators, 'a trace upon the waters', is the former President, George Bush. He held a large number of very important positions in American public life before he became President, yet made little mark upon them or their governance. A charming man, he too was greatly assisted by the strength and personality of his wife, who in many ways seemed a much bigger and more impressive figure than he did. By contrast, just as US Senate House Leader Newt Gingrich found, so the former Italian Prime Minister, Silvio Berlusconi, must realize, that once your reputation slips, it takes years to climb back up into the public arena. Likewise, there is no doubt that the Prince of Wales, after revelations about his private life, will take a long time to climb back to the same position he once held in the British public's affections. It is difficult to build a good reputation. It is very easy to break one, and once you have a bad reputation, you may never recover from it. The American actor Bill Cosby, who on television portrayed the epitome of good black family life, was particularly hard-hit when the scandal in his private life was exposed.

You personally also need to plan well ahead to build you reputation. To begin with, you have to be quite clear in your own mind what your core objectives are. Ask yourself:

- What do you want and where are you going?
- Are you after some specific reward, salary rise or some other sort of satisfaction?
- Do you want to safeguard your existing position and job, or are you looking for an enhanced one?
- Are you trying to persuade people to adopt your way of working, or to obtain a specific decision?
- Apart from material gains, what are your less quantifiable goals?

It may well be that you are pursuing a number of the above objectives, some of which may not be the most obvious ones, since a successful person will often opt for a job that is stimulating and satisfying rather than one that merely offers increased wealth or salary. Even if you are totally honest, both within yourself and with other people, what you want and what you say you want may well differ. Just as politicians use 'full stop' words like Morality, Justice, Liberty and Honesty, so we all, when we are negotiating a position, use similarly emotive words in order to justify a strategy that we are advocating.

Your approach will largely depend on what type of individual you are: are you self-motivated, or do you prefer someone to inspire you to action? While such aspects of your character will often be seen more clearly by colleagues and friends than by you, in the course of your life you will nonetheless have developed some sense of where you score and where you are likely to fail. Headhunters tend to keep a list of the qualities which they are always looking for in candidates for their shortlists. How do you consider you rate on the following? Would you claim you are:

- A good motivator?
- Able to come up with new ideas?
- Able to bring about constructive change?
- Someone who challenges entrenched dogmas?
- An effective monitor of results?
- Above all, good at communicating in the goldfish bowl of public life?

Candidates for high office, whether in industry, the public sector or elsewhere, need to be able to play all those parts well. Can you?

When, How, Where, Who?

Once you are clear who you are, what you are good and bad at and what your aims are, what you are going to do about it? Setting out to present yourself in the best possible light, you have to choose both the *right level* at which to put yourself forward and to make sure that your *timing* is correct. There is no point in pushing a really wonderful idea if the people you are trying to persuade – let's call them the Decision Takers – are not the appropriate ones, or if they are, are in the middle of some enormous crisis or on the point of going off to enjoy some well-earned holiday. Holiday periods, incidentally, can be hazardous or full of opportunity, depending on how you play your hand. Even the best-run organizations are unsettled when understaffed. Key advisers are difficult to get hold of. Colleagues don't like to disturb each other with business matters, particularly over a festive season. Everyone is a bit off guard.

Apart from timing, the most successful negotiators and tacticians will also do a large amount of advance research to establish precisely what the Decision Takers they are targeting want, and then create for themselves what is called 'hidden demand', which basically means a demand for their services which really did not exist before they offered it. What they are doing in effect is creating an aura which says, 'You may not have realized it, but if these are your aims, you really cannot do without me.'

In the meantime you also need to analyse what any likely opposition to your position is. Who else is around who is in competition for that post or who can and may influence your Decision Taker more than you can? Such opposition is often far from obvious. Apart from your peer group and your immediate colleagues, there are a lot of other people out there who may have just as good a reputation as you. Any senior executive will weigh the various competing candidates or sources of advice, and may even relish creating conflict between you all in order to get the results they want. Your ploy has to be to try to neutralize as many channels of likely opposition as possible. On the other hand, as Machiavelli argued in his book *The Prince*, it is sometimes quite a good idea to foster some sort of perceived opposition to you and to your bosses, so that if you overcome it, you can enhance their perception of your status and abilities. Creating a threat where none exists is a strategy that is used daily in politics. But it is constantly there in business life as well, on the lines of 'if we don't cut costs by sacking our Sales Director, our competitors are going to eat us alive', when circumstances in the marketplace do not suggest this at all.

It is not just any identifiable opposition to your preferred course of action that you need worry about. Equally dangerous are the neutrals and fence-sitters who can be both a nuisance and tricky to handle. Among this usually negative group are those who tend to argue that precedent rules. They are of the 'OK, let's get out the file and see what we did last time' school, or else they wait to see whether your ideas are going to fly before jumping on your bandwagon.

One example of tactical timing is to force a decision through by creating a deadline, on the lines of 'if you want me to join your company, I want £100k per annum and I want to know by tonight'. That approach has its very obvious dangers, but deadlines, even artificial ones, are sometimes essential to get people to come to conclusions. You see this if you are selling a car or a house. You say that all bids must be in by a certain time and it concentrates the minds of potential purchasers. Experience shows that deadlines can also frighten people off, but nonetheless, in most day-to-day activities, they tend to work. In general, the less time you give people, without straying into brinkmanship, the less time they have to marshal their case. This leads on to an offshoot to the Primacy Effect in tactical timing, which is to try to set the agenda in any strategic discussion by being first off the mark. If you get your ideas up and running in front of everyone early on, it is often difficult to unseat you or them later, just as favourable arguments put forward at the beginning of a debate are harder to knock down, and the first serious offer in a takeover bid is usually difficult to resist. Any opposition beaten to the post is surprised, disorganized or unsettled, and will need time to get their act together, while you may well get away with what you want.

In negotiating and networking with close colleagues or competitors who come to know you well, the Primacy and Recency Effects will become blurred into the general long-term reputation which you build up *vis-à-vis* those with whom you are working. If people perceive you to be influential, wise, and of good judgement in an historical context, then they are more likely to take your advice or go along with your strategy on current matters. A reputation for being influential or skilled in some other way becomes a hard and fast fact until you put a foot wrong. Much depends, of course, on the field in which you are operating or have your standing in; if you are known to be an expert on stock-market fluctuations, it won't necessarily be a surprise to you if you are not perceived to speak with authority in a totally unrelated field such as buying and selling Old Masters or betting on a Derby winner.

Returning to the question of what is the right level to operate at, it may not be the top individual in an organization to whom you should go to present yourself or your case, since he or she may not be the real Decision Taker. For example, in most business life, it is usually better to go to a Managing Director rather than a Non-Executive Chairman, just you would avoid going direct to a Government Minister but first deal with his civil servants. While doing so, remember that an underestimated aspect of tactics is to choose the right location in which to operate. Where you make your sales pitch can be crucial. Generally speaking, it is better to act on your own territory or one with which you are highly familiar. This, in strategic warfare, is known as the territorial imperative; as in sport, away games are always harder to win.

Knowing Your Target

The success or failure of any negotiation depends not only on assessing yourself, but also on assessing your target Decision Taker correctly. This is usually a subconscious process which anyone in business goes through several times a day. That Decision Taker may be a potential employer, a boss, a colleague, or even a junior whom you want to persuade to some course of action. You have to prepare a mental dossier on that person before you begin. The things that you need to consider include:

- Comparative institutional status
- Their ability to influence others
- Their moral strength and their prejudices
- What resources and allies they have
- What anxieties they display
- Their relative strength of will
- Their perceived reputation in relation to all the above.

Risk takers sometimes may be easier to persuade than those who prefer the status quo. Those who are susceptible to flattery have to be handled in a different way from those who are much more hard-headed. There are many other things to look out for. For example, if your target is opinionated, fond of hearing himself talk, you may have to learn the art of being silent. You also need to be wary of the person who, because he didn't think of it or because you are not his candidate for preferment, tends to be against it, or you. Many people like that do not want to negotiate: they just want to get their own way. In such circumstances it is a mistake to think that problems can be solved by open discussion. Often it merely makes them worse, since public differences of opinion and special pleading often only lead to even more controversy.

Negotiating

Anyone can improve their tactical abilities to negotiate, either for-mally or informally, when positions, policies or contracts have to be finalized, by learning how to use levers of all sorts, how to bargain, how to horse-trade. The key is always to watch out for what might be going on behind the scenes or could go wrong: the downside. This includes watching *your own* downside and being alert to when your influence is on the wane or being eroded. There is little to be gained by forcing matters to a head when received opinion is firmly against you, or wasting time on those whose ears are closed. Then you should start looking for a new job, a new Decision Taker on whom to practise your skills, a new world to conquer. In other words, if you find that doors are closing in front of you and your telephone calls are going unanswered, go gracefully. Don't cling.

In any strategic discussions within or between companies, there tend to be three basic types of negotiator:

1. The hard tactician who plays his hand as if it were a constant battle to win.
2. The soft touch, who gives and takes, always trying to seek a compromise.
3. The negotiator who conducts the whole process in terms of seeking mutual gain for both sides.

Research has turned up a number of other key qualities found in a really skilled negotiator. These include:

- Knowing how to assess the opposition and anticipate its plans, needs and fall-back positions.
- Knowing how to assess the opposition's strengths, weaknesses and allies. Who really are the most important participants in the negotiation?
- Knowing how to stress the advantages to the target Decision Taker of a given course of action and how to play down the benefits to yourself.
- Knowing how to get the timing right and not revealing your own views too early.
- As an extension to this, knowing how to play the 'creative use of silence' card. In a crucial discussion, if you do not talk, the other person feels they have to. At the Foreign Office we used to say that the best diplomat was someone who thought twice before saying nothing. Silence is even better than asking questions if the mood is right; it is always a hard argument to counter. Your opponents will give away their thoughts, approach, opinions, strategy. Talk less, learn more.
- Having an ability to bluff, short of having it called.
- Knowing how to employ the threat of a breakdown in negotiations, but always avoiding it in the end.
- Knowing how to use side issues to take the heat off or to distract attention.
- Knowing how to use psychological pressures. The American equivalent of Balliol's 'effortless superiority' characteristic was John F. Kennedy's 'grace under pressure': the ability to make people listen to you without raising your voice or demanding to be heard.

- Knowing how constantly to question your opponent's position when you are under attack.
- Knowing when to back off and when to put the pressure on.

Who is making the running here?

Negotiating in Committee

'Meetings are indispensable when you don't want to do anything.'

J.K. Galbraith

Most people believe that meetings are by and large a waste of time – 'taking minutes and wasting hours', as the old saying goes. The majority of British executives I know argue that they spend at least half their time in meetings, both formal and *ad hoc*. Some are indeed irrelevant. But meetings happen and they can be used. You may not want to go to them, but you certainly do not want to be left out. Handling your participation well can make a huge difference to your Primacy Effect, since frequently they are the only opportunities for some of your colleagues to see you interrelating in a working environment.

Companies and organizations hold meetings for lots of reasons. They hold them because they want to share information or find out what's going on, because individuals can't take a decision on their own, because they want to shelve the matter, or because they want to be there when a fundamental decision is taken. With this in mind, your aim, both in amicable and confrontational meetings and committees, should be to hold centre stage when you want to, make an impact when you choose, and keep your presence felt all the time, even when you are not talking. By choosing the right time to make an intervention, you avoid being interrupted or ignored. Neutralizing people who try to dominate or intimidate keeps a meeting both productive and focused on what is required. If all this sounds rather obvious, take care. Many strange plots are hatched to stitch up meetings, along with the more accepted methods of committee work such as people genuinely trying to achieve a compromise or a unanimous agreement on something. A great deal of careful preparatory work, good briefing papers, and a chairman who tries to avoid unnecessary clashes and keeps to the agenda, make for a successful meeting.

Over years of study, I have drawn up several apparently cynical but, I can assure you, deadly serious tactics which committee men and women use to advance their causes:

- Making sure most key decisions are taken before or out of committee. In boardrooms where there is a powerful chairman, the last thing he will want is a serious debate which might result in things not going his way.
- Making sure that the membership is properly balanced, a fact well appreciated by public companies who appoint non-executive directors to sit on their boards, to give a broader perspective and the right impression to the outside world.
- Ensuring the committee is of the right size. It is no new thought that the productivity of a board of directors is in inverse proportion to the number of members on it.
- Persuading the chairman of something in advance. Always agreeing with him in public.
- Filling up the agenda with routine. We all know that time spent on a subject is often in inverse proportion to its importance. This is a very serious tactic indeed.
- Ensuring, if it is going to be difficult to reach a decision on something, that the item is the last one on the agenda, then forcing it through against a time deadline.

- Otherwise watching and using the clock closely.
- Making absolutely sure who has the last word over what the minutes say. A clever chairman will lead off with: 'Let me summarize what we agreed' or 'This is what we have decided . . .' When it comes to the written minutes, the technique of fractionally altering them, known in Whitehall as 'marginal drafting', it is a peculiar skill much used by company secretaries and civil servants, and can be discerned only by the most painstaking. Few people read minutes. Fewer people challenge them. Almost no one remembers precisely what was actually agreed.

If you feel that all this is rather fanciful and that real people don't behave in this way, you are wrong. A British government booklet, *Guidance on the Exercise of the Presidency*, prepared for one recent UK Presidency of the European Community and later leaked to the press, included these gems on how to manipulate meetings:

> The UK's objective may be to delay a decision (e.g. until after the UK Presidency). As long as the UK is not isolated, the simplest device will be for the chairman to let delegations ramble on.

> Provided that agreement is not actually staring him in the face, he may be able to conclude that a number of new issues have been raised which require consideration in capitals and reflection by the Commission.
>
> When the day comes to resume, the meetings can then be cancelled because another group needs the meeting room . . . and so on.

It even suggested one very useful piece of discreet collusion:

> It is not uncommon for the national delegation (i.e. Britain) to take an extreme position at one end of the spectrum, leaving the Presidency scope for an apparently even-handed compromise which is actually highly acceptable to the national delegation.

With such clever thinking, there is obviously scope for British diplomacy yet.

Out-of-Committeemanship

Amid all this drivel (in committee) the useful men present, if there are any, exchange little notes that read, 'Lunch with me tomorrow – we'll fix it then'.

C. Northcote Parkinson

Parkinson's Out-of-Committeemanship is an important tool. When he wrote about it, it was largely treated as a joke. But it is not humorous; it is deadly serious. Such tactics daily ensure that most meetings or committees only rubber-stamp decisions which have already been fixed in the anterooms, the clubs, or over a good lunch well before the meeting itself. Skilful out-of-committee fixers win hands down. They know their allies and opponents and encourage or neutralize them in advance. They will, for example, get an ally to ask the all-important question, to urge delay, to pick an argument, or to be aggressive or conciliatory. They know the precise psychological moment to say nothing at all. They are astute in recognizing these skills in others and bypassing them. Discretion and the wisdom of operating behind closed doors is a key qualification. The most successful committee and out-of-committee people are those who open their mouths in public least but are second to none in whispering words in antechamber ears.

As an aside, I know one powerful and influential diplomat who always gets his way in casual discussions, in plenaries and in committees, but who loses out on his written material because reason, logic and presentational skills seem to desert him as soon as he puts pen to paper. He cannot produce a discussion paper without overwriting, over-explaining and taking ten pages where one would suffice. There are three rules for written communications: brevity, clarity and a good layout which catches the eye and focuses the reader's attention on the main points. Give the headlines, fill in the story, summarize at the end. One of the most successful of all negotiators I've ever known has the habit of distributing, at the start of a committee meeting, a single sheet of A4 setting out *his* main points. Even those who have not had time to read the committee working papers will read this. He infuriates chairmen and company secretaries, but he has set the agenda more firmly than the agenda paper itself.

Board Meetings

Very few boards stop to consider their own competence and effectiveness. Company board meetings ought to enhance the success of a business, yet, in many companies, such meetings are viewed as an administrative irrelevance. Except for legal reasons, there is no point in having them unless their objectives are well established in advance and the whole structure, timing and length of them, and how strongly they are led or chaired, are understood from the outset. Boards have to be fully informed about what is going on, and as a result board papers should be circulated well in advance of any meeting, ensuring the right balance between discussion time and routine agenda items. As always, one of the key issues is who sets that agenda. Those who control what is going to be discussed control the outcome and the performance of a company for a long time to come.

The timing, location and length of board meeting are also crucial. Management statistics seem to show that most company board meetings last about three hours, but so much depends on the business in hand. Too many board meetings follow some outdated, predetermined ritual, which, by definition, challenges the very effectiveness of them. The degree of pressure under which the board is operating will also determine how much effect you as an individual can have at them. If there is a crisis in the air, then the likelihood of you being able to put a point across or get a position accepted is correspondingly reduced. Despite what people may have thought was an almost light-hearted section above on out-of-committeemanship, my experience has overwhelmingly been that most serious discussion and decision-taking takes place well before the board meeting itself. As a further aside, my own view is that serious long-term strategy meetings ought to be held quite separately from board meetings, and are almost always much more effective if they take place well away from the usual boardroom in some neutral surroundings.

If you are the chairman, much will depend on your skill in building the board into a team that works together rather than as antagonists. The whole question of team-building and teamwork is beyond the scope of this book, but a good chairman will ensure that meetings are well structured and ordered without being too rigid. He or she will have worked out how much time should be allocated to each item on the agenda and will have decided which particular members of the board can most helpfully contribute to any given item of discussion. Some chairmen believe that a good team is a good team doing what they say. Others realize that the only real point in having board members present at a committee meeting is to give breadth and depth to the debate. Otherwise, why are they there? The quality, presence, charisma, gravitas and general authority of the chairman, ideally with all the attributes and qualifications and ability to communicate that we have discussed in earlier chapters, are crucial.

Networking

As we saw right at the beginning, life is all about relationships. You may have the best Primacy Effect and your communication skills may be outstanding, but who are you applying them to? The phrase 'Old Boy Network' gives a slightly pejorative tone to the very serious subject of who you yourself should network with in order to get a job, find people for jobs, or reach decisions in your present position. There is absolutely nothing seedy or under-the-carpet about networking. It is a perfectly legitimate way of arriving at decisions with like-minded people without going through the often long-winded and time-consuming formalities of a structured organization's decision-taking process. It happens at all times at all levels in all walks of life. People are appointed in this way to the highest levels of government, to the chairmanships of quangos, to the boards of public companies, to professorial chairs in universities, and to roles and ranks at every other level of life. A networking system exists in this country as it exists in almost every other country in the world. In China, for example, the whole question of networking is far more advanced than it is in the United Kingdom. It is nothing to be ashamed of. It is what makes for good appointments, it speeds up decision-taking, it helps form the best strategies.

We all network all the time. We deal with people we like and with people we know as much as we possibly can, in preference to dealing with people we dislike or people who are strangers to us. No matter how unselfish we are – and people working for aid and charity organizations, or fund-raising campaigns, are past masters at such string-pulling – we automatically create a network of mutual indebtedness and self-interest, trading in contacts to the best of our abilities. Networks are the webs which inform and hold together the machinery of any country, industrially, politically and commercially. Recognizing this important core fact, you should structure your tactics to get the best advantage for you out of such a system.

You have to build up your own network. You may not realize it, but you have the makings of one already, and all that I advocate is that you organize it in a much more structured way. If you are looking for a job, for example, it would be absurd not to draw up a list of all the contacts you have in the various companies and organizations which might have an interest in employing you. While these contacts may not be the actual Decision Takers on whether or not you get interviewed for such and such a position, you can still let them know that you are available or could be available. If they like you or respect you, in all probability they will keep their eyes open and do what they can to help when the right slot opens up. I have always suggested keeping a little black book of names and phone numbers, because, ever since I became a headhunter, I found that one of the basic problems facing me or any recruitment specialist (one that does not always occur to the man or woman in the marketplace looking for a job), was that I simply did not know who all the people were out there who might prove good candidates on the right terms and conditions. The marketplace for labour is a highly imperfect one. The whole basis of networking is to make sure that it becomes more perfect, by not just waiting for a job advertisement to appear, but by telling the potential employer that you are ready and waiting if the circumstances match. There is nothing wrong with that. Networking helps ensure that you, your light and the bushel are always visible and available.

'How d'you think that meeting went?' the Chairman asked Dr Mackenzie as they left the boardroom.

'Not bad, JD,' she responded, 'though I thought you let Bill talk too much.'

'He's good, isn't he?'

'He's getting better,' said Ruth Mackenzie, 'but two or three other people round that table – well I didn't know why they were there. Didn't open their mouths.'

'I should insist that everyone speaks?'

'You should certainly encourage them so to do, otherwise why have them there?' said Ruth Mackenzie briskly.

'A couple I didn't want to hear speak. If I'd let them, they would have rambled all over the place. And, besides, most of the decisions, as you know, were already taken. The Board was merely rubber-stamping.'

Ruth Mackenzie shrugged. 'That's the way of board meetings. Incidentally, if I were you, I would have let the Company Secretary deal with more of the routine things. You should hand all these purely technical and legal matters, financial statements and so on, to those responsible. A chairman should keep his role for the major issues. There's also the morale aspect – letting the Company Secretary know that he's wanted.'

The Chairman sighed, 'OK, OK. I suppose I asked for that.'

'You did ask me, Sir,' responded Ruth Mackenzie. 'I was doing a lot of antennae work, noting how the others around that table reacted to you. When that advertising team came in to do their pitch, for example, half the Board were paying attention and the other half were dreaming about an evening with their wives or girlfriends.' She paused. 'By the way, you do realize...?'

'What now?' asked the Chairman.

'The Financial Director got off very lightly with his very shaky bottom-line figures?'

'I'd already pulled him apart on that.'

'Yes, but the rest of the board ought to have had time to hit him around as well. The way that the agenda was structured meant there was no time to give him the attention he was due before we broke for lunch.' She paused, then asked, 'You know why?'

'Tell me,' said the Chairman.

'A little bird told me that the Finance Director got at the Company Secretary and asked, for the most innocent reasons, for the agenda to be changed so that the financial section he was most worried about came just when it did.'

'That's what I call clever,' said the Chairman thoughtfully. 'Maybe I've been under-valuing that man after all,' he said.

ASSESSMENT GROUP EXERCISE

JOB SPECIFICATION

Head of Strategic Planning, International Communication Group

METHOD OF APPOINTMENT

A board decision was recently taken to recruit from within the Group, since it was felt that experience of company procedures and culture was likely to be of more relevance to this particular appointment than skills parachuted in from outside.

A group of six middle managers and strategic analysts from a variety of different nationalities and backgrounds, but all fluent in English, drawn from Group Offices in the UK, the US, Europe, the Far East and Australasia, were selected. They were given a number of written, oral and practical tasks to perform over a two-day period, in an out-of-town hotel. They were monitored by two senior staff members and one external communications consultant.

MONITORING GROUP REPORT

Herewith a summary of the findings of the report. Detailed commentary on each candidate can be obtained if required.

At the outset, the six, two women and four men, all in their mid to late thirties, all with reportedly high-class minds and outstanding work experience within the Group, were, at the outset, judged by the monitoring team as having roughly equivalent skills and aptitudes for this key position. For all of them, the playing field was, therefore, level as they began the first exercise.

By the end of the first morning a variety of different interrelationships had built up. The opening exercise, where the six had to work as a group on a crisis-management case study, identified five who were happy to bond in this way and one, a total loner, who, though very bright, sat on the sidelines and tended to snipe. Throughout the next 24 hours, this candidate, who is, apparently, a brilliant backroom researcher, ruled himself out of the running. He projected a poor personal image, communicated only grudgingly, and while he could be acerbic and funny, could never hold the respect of any team.

The second written and oral exercise, in the unanimous view of the monitoring team, weeded out two more: one woman and one man. The woman tended to talk too much, interrupting all the time, and was very reluctant to let the others get a word in. Even when the other candidates were making their case, her whole body language expressed either disinterest or boredom. At dinner later and at other social events, she continued to try to hog the limelight and the others rapidly isolated her. The man failed the second exercise for the simple reason that he made no contribution whatsoever to the debate. Even when encouraged by the monitoring staff to speak, he would do so in a manner that was confused and boring. He marshals his thoughts very well in writing and it is on that that his reputation stands. He fails dramatically with the spoken word and he appears to recognize this, since he sits or stands, bent like a much older man, as if embarrassed by his own performance.

This left three who, because we did not want to have to break up the whole group until the end of the exercise in case the rejects suddenly appeared with massively redeeming features, we managed to sidetrack on to a separate exercise so that we could watch how they fared when they were pitted against each other. This worked very well, and so did they as a team, each contributing significantly to the exercises which they were set. What did emerge, however, was that one of the two men is a natural leader. He set both the time schedule and the agenda for tackling the exercise, yet did so almost without his two colleagues noticing. He got them working together rather than against each other, naturally 'chairing' their discussions, separating the wheat from the chaff, then summarizing the conclusions at the end. But, most importantly, when it came to presenting the group findings to the monitoring team and it was he who stood up to make their case. This he did courteously and well, with modesty, good humour and a great deal of natural generosity towards the input into the solution made by his two colleagues. Watching the latter as he stood up to make the presentation, their body language and the good rapport he had with them made it seem as if they wanted him to succeed, which he did. He has a great future ahead of him.

CHAPTER 8

Going for Influence Rather than Power

Getting your own way

Speech is power: speech is to persuade, to convert, to compel.
Ralph Waldo Emerson

The renown of great men should always be measured by the means which they used to achieve it.
La Rochefoucauld

Corrupt influence is itself the perennial spring of all prodigality and of all disorder: which loads us more than millions in debt; which takes away vigour from our arms, wisdom from our councils and every shadow of authority and credit from the most venerable parts of our constitution.
Edmund Burke

It's the hinge that squeaks that gets the grease.
Malcolm X

You can stroke people with words.
F. Scott Fitzgerald

There is an understandable tendency for ambitious people seeking a new job or promotion to aim for appointments that appear to offer them authority, prestige and power. But, as any senior civil servant will tell you, going for high-level positions of influence behind the scenes can be just as satisfying and rewarding. In any event, Prime Ministers and their colleagues in the Cabinet, as well as so-called Captains of Industry and most other high-profile leaders, seldom have real, unfettered power in any case. They are subject to the same sorts of restraints as the rest of us. Those who have polished up their Primacy Effect and know how to use it win the day in the influence stakes.

Powerful people are seldom what they seem. Those with apparent responsibility, that is those who hold some formal position in any hierarchy but do not have the sanctions or force of personality necessary to force through what they want, are all around us. A lot of men and women who are said to be powerful are, in effect, simply holders

He appeared to have power, but it was in chains

of authority slots, while the real decisions are taken by people with influence, working from behind the scenes. Such individuals include the strategists and agenda setters, the spin-doctors, private secretaries and speech-writers, who actually make things happen.

Another way of looking at the difference between power and influence is to recognize that in any organization there is a system to be worked. We may think that there is a given chain of command. It may all be set out in black and white on the notice-boards at company headquarters, but we all know perfectly well that a direct line between the chairman, his personal secretary and one or two key figures in the organization often bypasses the basic administrative structures and pecking orders. It happens in most walks of life. An alert analyst of decision-making patterns looks first at the chairman or tycoon's right-hand man or woman, their closest advisers, even their spouses. Knowing the membership of a 'Kitchen Cabinet' and their inter-relationships, means knowing where any system most effectively gets to work. Look at successive British Governments: in No. 10 Downing Street in the period from Margaret Thatcher to Tony Blair, for example, the policy staff were and are far more important than most supposedly powerful Cabinet Ministers.

The End of Power

Because of the constraints on real power, which was once defined by Bertrand Russell as 'an unfettered ability to achieve intended effect', it rarely exists, least of all in modern democratic societies. Absolute power is almost totally unheard of. Despots are out. The influential are in. This is because social, political, ecological and moral constraints are so prevalent and act so decisively on all leaders in all walks of life that the people whom the headline-writers call powerful are seldom that. In varying degrees top men and women are in the business of either buying obedience or offering patronage.

We have all, of course, met people who have an aura of power about them, but this tends to be largely to do with the awe in which their staff hold them and stems more from their ability to take certain decisions within their own limited empire. Yes, to that extent, they have power. Outside that empire, however, they are severely limited. This is why more and more intelligent and ambitious people seek to influence and persuade and otherwise gain the ability to change events or the minds and decisions of others without bothering with having the formal authority to do so. Influence has replaced power-seeking as the goal of the would-be élite.

Look at it another way. For all kinds of reasons we delude ourselves into accepting most public and commercial decisions and courses of action as if they were resolved by one person or a single body in authority. There are many misconceptions about the nature of position and authority. We are particularly impressed by titles, even though they prove nothing. Phrases such as 'the Prime Minister has decided ...' or 'the Chairman and Board have ruled ...' are commonplace inaccuracies. What these individuals have often done is merely to rubber-stamp what the executives much further down the tree have already implemented. By using expressions such as 'one of the most powerful men in the country today', however, we continue to sustain the impression that there is still a commodity around called effective power. This ignores the subtler reality that even a Chief Executive seldom has complete freedom to make a decision and to ensure that it is carried out, because of a whole plethora of internal and external restraints. This is because we sometimes mistake for power the personal driving force which many top industrialists possess. As we will see from the Case Study at the end of this chapter, while they can make things tick within their sphere of influence, they can seldom, even if they present well, affect their company's share price. The energy and determination of one person can without question transform an organization, but in the long term an autocratic organization dies when the constraints that exist in a wider corporate society take their grip.

In the real world, therefore, those who are conventionally branded as having the ability to take this or that course of action, those who appear to be in the driving seat and with whom the buck may indeed have to stop (particularly if something goes wrong) seldom possess total freedom of action. The reality is that power everywhere is in chains. Harold Macmillan said it very concisely: 'Power is like a Dead Sea fruit. When you achieve it there is nothing there.'

Theorists, historically, have considered three forms of power: raw physical power or brute force – the power of the thug in a street fight; legal, military or disciplinary power, in which the right to coerce is built into the system; and financial power, which operates indirectly as a sanction. This latter relationship, which is the usual employer–employee one, is where the ability to compel obedience is solely via a threat to withhold reward. It forces compliance by saying in effect, 'If you do not do what I say, I will stop paying you.' Such relationships tend to be executive and are easy to spot. We see the clenched fist or the loaded pistol; we know the power of a drill sergeant; if we have a piper on our payroll we are entitled to tell him what tunes we want to hear. Nominal power exists wherever formal authority exists, although the exercise of that power almost always is diluted to take account of the views of others.

Power and Influence

What has this Power/Influence relationship to do with the Primacy Effect and your own ability to convince others of your own worth and that of the ideas or strategies you are pushing? It is very simple. Even if you don't sit in or near the top seat, by utilizing your personal impact skills cleverly you can change the decisions taken by those in apparent authority over you. You may already act like this without realizing it. Think of the relationship between power and influence as a spectrum, with power at one end and influence at the other. Power still exists, for example in a Managing Director's executive function. Influence on the other hand depends on the ability of you and your colleagues to persuade, irrespective of your rank. In the real business world, the power part of the spectrum is very short indeed and is subject to a huge range of financial or institutional blockages. There is a middle band, where power and influence overlap or co-exist, but to the right of that band is where the much more exciting area of influence begins, where you, while lacking the means to force through a single course of action, can use your personal impact skills and other stratagems to achieve your ends.

While many employees think they have an autocrat as a boss, even dictators have to modify their actions in reaction to external events or in anticipation of how the ruled may react if pushed too far. Influence, by contrast, is the lubricant of the decision-taking process. It can vary from a persuasive whisper in the boss's ear to, say, a full-scale campaign to convert your fellow workers. There are lots of ways of getting someone to work, to run or to stop without using a stick or other blunt instrument. Influence can be positive or negative, depending on what you want someone to do and what they think of you. A reputation for being influential sharply increases your prominence on the influence spectrum. You are influential only if you are perceived so to be.

The first Baron Acton, who is best known for having coined the adage 'Power tends to corrupt and absolute power corrupts absolutely' in an age when absolute power was much more common, went on: 'Great men are almost always bad men even when they exercise influence and not authority ... There is no worse heresy than that the office sanctifies the holder of it.' Recent events in and around the White House certainly go a long way towards giving substance to this and underline the constant need to try to disentangle the exact way in which influence working on 'authority' produces a particular result.

In the past, influence was also characterized by political theorists as a property or possession, which could be won, lost, appropriated or given away. Looked at in this way, the struggle for influence in the courts, chancelleries and boudoirs became the central purpose of most social and political life. However, it cannot and never could exist in a vacuum – a relationship is necessary to bring it into being, and now, as then, your effectiveness is totally dependent on your relationship with the person you are trying to influence. To a large extent it will also be circumscribed by a whole set of external and subordinate relationships. As always, it is no good trying to influence someone unless timing and circumstances are right.

Influence comes in various forms, but there are two basic types: micro-influences and macro-influences. Micro-influences are direct forms of influence, one person to another, you to me, where you use all your political, moral, social, religious, monetary, commercial, diplomatic, cultural, intellectual, ideological and/or sexual guile to win your case. Micro-influences also have to take into account macro-influences, which are a whole host of external pressures, including public opinion, political stability levels, the state of competition legislation, the availability of scarce resources and a huge range of other constraints. Things that change attitudes or thinking or company policy can be as permanent and inevitable as Britain's weather, or as short-term as the government's current economic thinking. Transient influences come and go. Today's good cause, hairstyles, skirt lengths and similar social whims and ephemeral fads make the person you are trying to influence as subject to the pressures of everyday life as anyone else. You may think, incidentally, that when you are attempting to influence someone you yourself will remain unchanged, but your target will also be influencing you in return, if only in the way in which you feel you should present your case to them. At a more competitive level, you don't operate alone and have to react and interreact with influential colleagues, opponents, deputies and friends.

The degree to which you are influential also depends on what is called your potential/effective ratio. A father may have great say over what his children do. He may not wish to use it, however, because of the restraints imposed on him by his desire for domestic harmony, his fear of what the neighbours might say, whether he's tired, what's on television and so on. In addition to that, he may actually decide to conserve any authority he has, keeping it in reserve for extreme circumstances. A variant of this, which further emasculates so-called power, is called the Perceived Authority Factor. This works as follows. A managing director may wish all his employees to buy British cars, but he may decide not to insist on it as he knows there is little likelihood of his being obeyed. His realization that his authority is limited and may be opposed results in him not making the demand in the first place. In other words, rather than throwing down a gauntlet, he restrains himself and thereby avoids a possible defeat that would weaken his apparent position. He takes a weak stand now so that he may appear stronger in the future. We all do this all the time. We don't push a case too hard, in order to retain our influence for a later occasion.

Influence and Persuasion

Look at how the influence you are hoping to achieve works in practice.

We have all seen it happen. Some great public figure adjusts his spectacles and shuffles through the briefs on the table in front of him. As he leans forward and prepares to speak, he is almost masked by a battery of microphones. Television cameras zoom in to focus on him; pencils tap expectantly; shorthand pads flutter; eyes turn attentively. Then, anticlimax, hesitation. A grey-faced adviser from among the anonymous bunch seated in the row of chairs behind, leans forward to whisper in the great man's ear. After a moment or two of consultation, the great man nods and at last begins to speak.

What has happened? Some senior company executive, adviser, civil servant, commercial or PR confidant, totally unknown outside his own peer group and lacking the power to force the great public figure to take any particular line, has chosen his timing with Machiavellian cunning, to cause the words to be altered or amended. Anyone with experience of good executives or civil servants of any nationality will have come across this as an almost daily occurrence. The first thing that happens when a new government minister or company chairman takes up his office, for example, is that all those around him, private secretaries and others, will conspire and collude on how to work him in the future.

In political and commercial life there are continual attempts by large and small pressure groups to influence decisions. Petitions, demonstrations, rent-a-mobs and slogans are their tools. Enormous organizational skills and sums of money are called into play to mount them. Yet why do any number of shareholders or Greenpeace activists demonstrating at an AGM against fat-cat salaries or an impending environmental disaster only have nuisance value, while some unseen finance director or head of public affairs pulls the real levers? Why is it that a lone adviser may have incomparably more influence on the powers that be than all those demonstrating outside? What relationship exists between the great public figure and the whisperer in the row behind? The combination of time, place, interpersonal relationships, subject-matter and the interplay of various external influences is astutely manipulated by the inside team to influence what the company or organization eventually does. As I said earlier, whatever the management structure, there is always a hidden system that bypasses the proper channels of authority. You have to be in it to know it. A coterie of the Managing Director plus Bill plus Harry often outweighs the combined organizational might of the Chairman, the Board, and the Sales, Production and Development Directors put together.

How do you go about utilizing your skills and the perceptions that people have of you? Your target Decision Taker is the key. He or she is the wielder of authority, and the holder of the purse strings. But who exactly is it? The fundamental question to ask of any system is 'who is really in charge?' Is it really the MD? As we all know, any company has its quota of nominal managers, people who react or wait to see what others are going to do before moving. The person who matters, and whom you need to get to, is the Decision Taker, the creative spirit who knows how to circumvent the diversions and roadblocks of life. You, like them, have to identify the Pressure Points or Progress Points that stop or change the direction in which an organization is going, and identify who is really going to drive things forward as opposed to merely being in a title-holding role.

In using and building up your influence, always ask yourself the following questions:

- How good is the internal communication system (a) upwards and (b) downwards?
- How reliable is the information communicated?
- At what level are decisions made? Which are the other key levels of responsibility?
- Is decision taking confined to the top?
- What hidden patterns of leadership are there?
- Is the administration effective?
- Is nonconformity considered bad?
- Are bright subordinates listened to?
- Is competition rather than teamwork the order of the day?
- How much resistance to change is there?
- Above all, how much of an informal system is there that bypasses the formal decision-taking system?

The flatter any organizational structure is, and the less steep-sided the management pyramid, the easier it is going to be to identify your key Decision Taker. As with a piece of machinery, the more pieces there are, the more complex it is. By contrast, a tight organization has less need for a 'system' by which to operate.

Decision Making and Decision Taking

How you can personally inject your influence into such a system is really about two things: decision making and decision taking. You need not spend too much time on the latter. Life is, as we have seen, conveniently presented as if decisions are always taken by individuals in positions of formal authority. But that authority is never as great as it is formal. The president waving to the crowd, the company director whose signature is needed at the bottom of the document, the formal 'decision taker', may have made little active contribution to the process by which that decision was actually *made*. At the top of the tree, some industrial leaders are often relatively passive, powerless rather than powerful, more pawns for the influential than decision makers in their own right, with the real activity beavering away down below. There is a widespread belief that big business decisions are taken at the top after a cool analysis of the facts, on the basis of rational thought and calculated argument, carefully balancing the advantages and the disadvantages. Sadly, most commercial organizations are woefully confused in their thinking. Their information systems are hopelessly inadequate and their executive judgements are clouded by prejudice, ignorance, pride, stubbornness and a lot of other factors. They grope and stumble along ill-lit routes to reach conclusions that are often highly detrimental to themselves. Most important of all, makers and takers of decisions almost always allow themselves to reach a decision which is already framed by the language in which the problem has first been defined. History and precedent can be poor tutors or guides, and a decision that led to success or failure in the past is not necessarily right or wrong the second time around: the circumstances may have changed completely. In other words, the answer may be all right but the question may have been deplorably formulated. That's where you and your influence come in.

In rehearsing your options before you move in, with your tactical guns blazing, there are a number of simple questions you should ask yourself:

- Who is pushing what line?
- What is their motive?
- Is the strategy being framed within the right parameters?
- Are the alternatives genuine – or is the 'either you do this or you go bankrupt' argument a false one?
- Is your Decision Taker being pushed toward the too obvious solution?
- How many pet theories are there behind what has been proposed?
- Are they falling into the trap of being dictated to by past experience?
- What's the downside to you if your advice is rejected?

In order to utilize all your personal impact skills to best effect, you have to look at all possible solutions through a telescope as well as a magnifying glass. 'What's in it for me?' may sound like a very selfish approach to life, but as in most circumstances, you have to look after your own interests because no one else will do it so well, and, more charitably, you won't be able to help others, their strategies and their goals, from a position of personal weakness. The way to achieve personal satisfaction and a more profitable career is seldom to march up the full-frontal route. Hone up on your skills of influence and persuasion. The subtle way usually wins in the end.

'You're saying I have no power?' asked the Chairman, a trifle indignantly.

'You have authority,' said Dr Mackenzie, cautiously. 'You can hire me and fire me. You can insist that certain decisions are taken, but you know only too well the limits on what you can really achieve. You can talk your heart out to City analysts and fund managers, but you can't insist that they invest a penny in this company.'

'I am well aware . . . The shareholders scream if I do one thing, my fellow directors scream if I do another, the trade unions are regaining their strength . . . And that's not even taking my wife's views into consideration.'

'Betty, your secretary, always seems to have a pretty good idea what is going on.'

'Betty is a better behind-the-scenes communicator than any of us. I don't mean she's indiscreet. She just fixes things when she sees conflict coming along.'

'Which is the way it should be.'

'So it's all a game of influence, then, is it?' asked the Chairman.

'Put it this way, JD. Even in your wisest moments you're going to take advice from X rather than Y because you prefer X to Y rather than because you prefer his or her strategy.'

'Like the old adage about giving work to a busy man?'

'Sure, JD. If you perceive someone to be effective and influential, then they are effective and influential. You're subject to the same pressures, both micro and macro, as everyone else. There's nothing much you can do about the Chancellor's new corporation tax rates nor the downturn in the world economy. All you can do is react by trying to persuade the government that certain things are good for this company and certain things are bad. That's what influence is all about.'

'I must tell my wife just that,' said the Chairman, reflectively.

ROADSHOW ASSESSMENT

CONFIDENTIAL TO BOARD
REPORT BY MS ASSOCIATES ON MULTINATIONAL
PLC'S PROPOSED ROADSHOW TO INVESTMENT ANALYSTS AND
FUND MANAGERS

SPECIFICATION

MS (Financial PR) Associates has been retained by the Chairman and the Board to report on and suggest improvements to the financial and strategic team presentation that is to be given by senior executives in London, Edinburgh, Frankfurt, Zurich and New York.

REPORT

The Roadshow Team comprises the Chief Executive, Finance Director and General Manager. They are all of course highly knowledgeable about the business, wherein lies a commonly found failing: they are too close to the day-to-day issues and have a less than clear view of, firstly, how much they need to tell their audiences and, secondly, what these highly specialized audiences want to know. These two objectives are not similar.

The Company has been going through a bad patch and press comment has been indifferent or poor, which has been reflected in the low share price. The underlying strengths of the Company are substantial and the latest interim figures good. The problem is one of perceived management strength and getting that across to an unconvinced market.

As is not uncommon, one of the three Roadshow members was cynical about the need for any presentation training. He believes his slides and other audio-visual material should be sufficient for the purpose.

MS Associates has now sat in on two full-scale rehearsals. The first was a total disaster: no one had prepared, the texts of the three contributors were confused and unstructured, and the Chief Executive delivered most of what the General Manager's section was meant to contain. There were far too many slides and the majority of these were badly set out.

In particular, the Finance Director's contribution was merely to read out, badly, what was already up on the screen, which everyone else had read in detail before he was finished.

We were allowed to take away and reunite all three texts into a coherent whole. We translated the often indecipherable verbiage of the 'Company Chinese', in which it was written, into language that is much less complex and easier to deliver in spoken English by the participants. We simplified and cut back the number of slides by half, and have prepared additional key information in printed form, to be handed out to those attending the Roadshows.

We then took each member of the team individually through his contribution. As there is considerable rivalry between them, we kept our more forceful criticisms for these private sessions. The Chief Executive is a very incisive figure but appears languid, even laid back, when he speaks. The Finance Director has a delivery style like a speaking-clock machine, while the highly ambitious General Manager is highly strung, red-faced and perspiring, always looking as if he is about to have a heart attack.

The second rehearsal was much more successful, and because they all knew it went well, this on its own has added to their confidence and to their realization that they need to be seen to be working as a team. All three have begun to learn to avoid most of their presentational faults, and though there is still much ironing out to be done, they are all aware that the style and authority of their delivery, to a cynical audience that already has most of the figures, is crucial in establishing them as personalities who are determined to lead the Company and its share price back to where it rightfully belongs.

CHAPTER 9

The Feminine Challenge

Is there a glass ceiling?

Whatever women do they have to do twice as well as men to be thought half as good. Fortunately this is not difficult.

Anon

She wears her clothes as if they were thrown on her with a pitchfork.

Jonathan Swift

When a man gets up to speak, people listen, then look. When a woman gets up, people look; then, if they like what they see, they listen.

Pauline Frederick, US news correspondent

Remember Mary Archer in the witness box. Your vision of her will probably never disappear. Has she elegance? Has she fragrance? Would she have – without the strain of this trial – a radiance?

Mr Justice Caulfield

Afairly light-hearted study of attitudes among female high achievers in Britain recently revealed that a majority of them still feared being taken for a secretary and being asked to make the coffee. In consequence, such women were tending to dress down, in tailored suits, sensible shoes and subtle make-up. Too feminine, 'girly' looks were avoided in the never-ending bid to be taken seriously and achieve total parity with men.

Elsewhere, a recent article in the *Journal of the American Medical Association* reported Australian research which demonstrated that the brains of women are much better equipped for speaking than those of men. Specifically, the two areas of the brain associated with language are larger, which suggests that women should be more fluent speakers and have a better verbal memory. If these are true assumptions, any negative aspects of a woman's ability to communicate effectively must therefore be to do with such factors as body language, paralanguage and the stereotype perceptions that exist in what is still a largely male-dominated society. Society still has a strong aversion to accepting the authority of women in certain areas of activity. Affecting maleness as a solution does not, however, lead to effective femaleness.

The importance of image, impact and the Primacy Effect looms particularly large when we turn to the much-discussed subject of 'a woman's place' in business and public life. The common perceptions or mis-perceptions about women in offices are too familiar to need repeating here. What is the image or the truth? Do males see a female colleague as just another colleague, as a disruptive threat, as a challenge, or as a bit of light relief? How do career women balance toughness with femininity? Why can men more or less get away with a crumpled suit while a woman cannot get away with a ladder in her tights? Why, in a recent business survey, did most people, both male and female, believe that the chances of working for an effective woman boss are still fairly remote? Has the Primacy Effect got it wrong somewhere? Or was Margaret Thatcher correct when she said 'The cocks strut about and crow, but it's the hens that lay the eggs.' That said, most career women believe there is still a downside for them in the image game.

American television has inevitably spawned a number of well

known female faces of a variety of styles and attributes. At one end of the spectrum one has Barbara Walters, the veteran interviewer who has extracted as many confessions from famous faces as has, at another level, that black icon Oprah Winfrey. They have differing but equally successful approaches to sensationalizing the confessions of their interviewees. Both stand out well in comparison with Joan Rivers, whose entire *raison d'être* is to be shocking and to offend, which she does with great success. In total contrast with such media stars we have that paragon, that blast of fresh air at the State Department, Madeleine Allbright, a woman of great vim and vigour and also of erudition as befits a former Georgetown professor. She hits home with such telling phraseology as 'Problems abroad, if left unattended, will all too often come home to America.' Above all, she gets respect not just for the positions that she holds, but for what she is: a doughty, honest and vigorous supporter of world peace and diplomacy.

Women often feel they have a particularly hard row to hoe in gaining preferment or promotion over men. They believe they have to be especially alive to how they behave, dress and appear. Their public and private conversational styles, quite apart from their voice tones, become more important than men's. Women constantly have to take extra account of the prejudices of those around them, *including* other women, and have to develop additional skills in order to operate effectively and be treated seriously.

Perception rules: What is she really like?

One recent American management survey suggested that of all women who fail on the fast track, something like 35 per cent come unstuck because of their poor outward appearance alone, compared with a mere 5 per cent of men held back by a similarly poor public image. Here I am specifically not talking about 'looks' or the Halo Effect. Good looks for both men and women, especially extreme good looks, can be a real trap for both sexes in the advancement stakes. There is also a strong assumption in the inevitably male-dominated selection process, that no way can you be an intelligent and extremely good-looking woman *and* fit the bill.

A lot of evidence suggests that the most cynical and cautious of employers, again both male and female, are wary about putting a woman into certain sensitive jobs carrying specific degrees of authority. Managers worry that in the event of a conflict or a disagreement, it will inevitably be translated into some sort of gender war, in which every trivial social failing will be used as ammunition. On dress, in particular, men can simply climb into the same well-pressed pin-striped suit day after day after day. Provided they don't let their ties get too stained, they get away with it. Meanwhile, if a woman were to dress similarly day after day, she would soon be branded in disparaging terms. At the other extreme, if she sports a splendid change of outfit every morning, week after week, similar criticisms will all too easily be thrown. Hairstyle, fashion, amount of make-up, jewellery, neckline, skirtline – all these things are apparently trivial but critical traps for the unwary, the only solution being that so long as you are aware of them and take advice as well as using normal good sense, then the worst of the pitfalls can normally be avoided.

Gender Prejudice

What a woman can never totally climb over, however, is hidden, unspoken prejudice, where office politics really have turned into sexual politics. In the workplace or at meetings, the male of the species can be assertive or languid, cool or testy, determined or laid back. Women operating or speaking in similar ways will instantly bring pejorative adjectives down on themselves. Be assertive and you get the reputation for being too bossy, languid becomes dull or weak, determined becomes bloody-minded, and laid back – well, becomes laid back. For the deeper voices of the sort Margaret Thatcher trained herself into adopting, suggesting more maturity and authority than higher-pitched, more feminine tones, the critics still lie in wait.

No matter how polished a woman's Primacy Effect, she may come up against the so-called Glass Ceiling, above which women are not meant to be able to rise. It may not be visible, but it still exists in many organizations. Those who deny this quote the rise in the number of women leaders in so many countries around the world. But on examination, most of those great names tend to be found not in business and commercial life but in political life, where the selection process has been the democratic, secret ballot, and so the stereotype is not fully laid to rest. There is no question, however, that in certain areas of activity, for example in public relations, advertising, publishing and the media, women nowadays hold positions equal to or superior to those of their male colleagues.

Attraction and Advancement

As visual image is believed to play a particularly important part in gender issues, we inevitably come on to the dangerous subject of sexual attraction. As we saw at the beginning of the book, the primitive dictates of our nature determine what we find attractive in life generally. A beautiful view, a beautiful object, a beautiful picture, a beautiful man or woman, will gain our attention more easily than something ugly. The Halo Effect argues that good looks bring other fair qualities with them. The male of the species has often tried to determine what women find irresistible in them – hair or lack of it, big noses, small noses, tallness, smallness, big foreheads, small foreheads and so on have all been claimed, usually by their owners, to be attractive to others. In practice, anthropological and psychological studies have shown that eyes, lips, expressions and hidden body odours or pheromones all add to the appeal. Equally, hair colouring – blonde, brunette, red, even grey hair – can be attractive to some members of the opposite sex. American tests suggest that both genders are more attracted to symmetrical faces, the implication being that at a subconscious, primitive level, regular physical features are seen as a measure of biological quality. A genetic pairing with a member of the opposite sex with attractive features therefore offers the partner potentially good-quality offspring. There is also a downside, for research goes on to suggest that too attractive physical attributes and facial characteristics tend to lead to infidelity, both socially and in the workplace, because the well endowed, be they male or female, can choose and attract mates and workmates with greater ease that those physically and facially less gifted. Yet again, a lot of evidence suggests that attractive physical features do give an individual a head start in life, if only by boosting the possessor's internal confidence.

This is not the place to go into the whole subject of designer smells in the gender wars. Suffice it to say that a surprising amount of research has been done of injecting expensive leather smells into car showrooms and good coffee smells into grocery departments, so presumably the huge scent and fragrance market, which is increasingly directed at the male of the species as well, must be based on something more than just marketing hype.

Make Up or Make Down?

If you are not physically or facially particularly well endowed, what can you do about it? Does it really matter? Male and female fashion magazines are full of advice and tips about 'colouring yourself beautiful'. We all know examples of gifted, ugly people, who have huge allure, building up an attractiveness through the way they dress and deport themselves. The French call such a woman 'une jolie laide'. The whole question of make-up, for example, as part of the 'uniform' or dress women wear to improve their appearance, again seems to have a huge relevance, given the vast amount of money cosmetic companies spend marketing and advertising their products. British Airways stewardesses are given strict instructions on what is appropriate for them, including the use of one of only three shades of lipstick.

But in most business life any rules about make-up or dress are unspoken ones. If you are a female banker in the City of London, it would probably be advisable not to wear startlingly red lipstick, while in an upmarket advertising agency, wearing no make-up at all might make you look conservative, dowdy or uncaring. Like it or not, those who look 'successful' and are well turned out gain more opportunities, while a real turn-off for an upwardly mobile woman in British business society is the Barbie Doll look, which is read as being tarty no matter what other qualities the woman concerned may have. Studies of Wall Street bankers go further and suggest that, in the United States, the Glass Ceiling, while still firmly in place, is much less so for those women who take a great deal of care to 'look the part'. Unfair though it is, we have all come across instances of women being criticized for wearing too much make-up or for paying too little attention to their appearance – that criticism often coming from men seriously in need of grooming themselves. In sum, the bad news is that, in largely patriarchal societies, women get judged and assessed far more in terms of pure appearance than men do. There is an unjustly thin line between too much and too little. It may be wrong; it may make women angry; but it is still a fact of life that has to be coped with, for there is no doubt that a woman who looks her best creates an aura of self-confidence that gives her an extra boost in a highly competitive world.

Incidentally, it is not just women who have to look to make-up for help. Any man who has been interviewed for television knows it would be foolish not to accept the invitation to be made up, if only to cover spots and to have his forehead powdered so that he doesn't shine under the heat from the arc lights. During the last General Election in Britain, several of the male party leaders had make-up people travelling with them permanently. There was a lot of professional skill involved in deciding what make-up to use: Tory politicians tended to need more make-up, as they appeared on television and at party rallies in front of blue backgrounds, while their Labour counterparts needed less against red. In the heat of battle and with exhaustion setting in, the pallor or the flush on cheeks had to be rectified to suggest continued, bristling good health. But John Major's particular make-up artist was no longer in attendance when he finally went on television to admit election defeat. His grey, exhausted appearance admitted that failure long before the final votes had been counted.

Looking Healthy

The importance of image and of looking the part in this televisual age is not just confined to appearances on television. Even the most masculine of people benefit from looking reasonably healthy. While we are not models about to go on the catwalk of life, the 'take me as I am' persona is instantly marked down from a distance for looking weedy and unhealthy. Both men and women who look healthy gain particularly strong plus points in the Primacy Effect stakes. While it is now medically incorrect to go around with too deep a suntan, someone bursting with obvious good health, not too overweight, with a clear skin and no bags under their eyes will appear a much more potentially satisfactory candidate for a job. A dark tan, by contrast, suggests vanity or someone who has had too much time or money on their hands. Yellowing complexions and matching teeth are turn-offs.

If you look healthy, then the causes that you espouse are perceived as healthy too. Anita Roddick, the founder of the Bodyshop, a company devoted to ecologically sound health products, would not do herself or her company any service if she went around looking ill and tired. Equally, Lord Hanson always used to say, when he was at the head of his great Anglo-American empire, that his shareholders expected him to look fit and well. He made sure he always did. He insisted that all his senior staff did so as well, even to the extent of taking an overweight employee to task or paying for a company tricologist since he felt that unhealthy hair, with accompanying dandruff, was a sure turn-off with any customer or audience. The fact that, in the last year of President Mitterand's leadership of France, he was desperately ill from cancer and looked so ill, added hugely to the feeling of powerlessness which beset the Republic over that critical period. He had long been a colossal figure astride the post-war European scene, but the fact that he was known to be physically ill meant that his political strength was also undermined, even though he appeared to keep a grip on much of what was going on right up to the end. By contrast, the lacklustre Jacques Chirac, denied his predecessor's charisma, has failed, in purely presentational terms, to offer the image that France needs to present in order to confront its current difficulties.

Just as bright red lips and long red nails will relegate most women to the Barbie/Bimbo camp, human resource specialists are always alert to the opposite. A total lack of make-up may be acceptable in academic circles and in places where you want to send out the message that you are too busy and important to bother about superficial details like that. Care, however, is needed to avoid merely looking butch. There is a downside risk everywhere you look. I have heard headhunters argue that a woman, meticulously turned out, made up and extremely well-dressed, might create a highly threatening image in many business environments and should thus be rejected. Another interesting survey, again in the United States, had a number of women send out two sets of their CV's to a large number of different companies. On one set of CVs the candidate's photograph showed her well made up, on the other with no make-up on at all. No prizes for guessing that a far larger number of interviews were offered in the former category.

Given that many women feel insecure about how they should look and the sort of image they should be projecting, the best solution is probably to work on an efficient, not too jazzy look. The real problem will always remain the question of whether someone is dressing in a way he or she believes to be sexually attractive, or to suit themselves alone. As they say, the choice is yours.

As a tailpiece, do women listen more intently to an attractive man, and vice versa? There is some psychological evidence, beyond the scope of this book, that suggests that, from an early age, because boys and girls are dressed and responded to differently, early experiences contribute to our behaviour patterns in later life. Female readers of this book may disagree, but there is a lot of evidence to suggest that when addressing others, particularly men, they tend to smile more, require less interpersonal space and touch more, use more head nods and engage in more eye-contact than males. For good or bad, women are also perceived to be more skilled at interpreting non-verbal behaviour in their colleagues and the Primacy Effect rules them as particularly vulnerable as both hunters and victims.

'I've learned a lot over the last few weeks,' said Bill cautiously. 'But since we're on to the question of a woman's image in the workplace, perhaps I can give my views for a change.'

'Go ahead,' said Ruth Mackenzie.

'You, for example,' Bill continued, bravely. 'You've got degrees from Oxford and Harvard. So what are you doing spending your time on all this? Wouldn't you rather be doing than advising?'

'I am doing as well as advising,' she replied, staring hard at him.

'Then there's the way you dress,' Bill hesitated.

'Out with it,' she retorted. 'I've been criticizing you all around the shop. Have your own back.' As she spoke, Bill thought he picked up a first brief sign of uncertainty.

'With your hair pulled hard back, that pinstripe suit and those horn-rimmed glasses . . .' He paused. 'D'you remember all those old Hollywood films where the guy takes the woman's glasses off and makes her let down her hair and then . . . wham bang.'

'What exactly are you suggesting?' Ruth Mackenzie blushed a little.

'Nothing and everything. You're practising what you teach, I suppose: power dressing for the role you have.'

'Which is what I set out to do. If we were going out for dinner, you would find me clothed very differently.'

'Is that an offer?'

'Ask and see.'

'Then there's your colour-coding,' said Bill, moving swiftly on. 'Autumn colours rather than bright pinks and reds. Do different people suit different colours?'

'What I think doesn't matter. Almost everybody prefers certain colours. More important are facial expressions . . . especially a woman's . . . Frozen expressions can be a turn-off . . . or a giveaway. As we go through life, our faces gradually pick up what we are like emotionally. Smiling or frowning, even on a young face will leave faint lines that can denote a temperamentally cheerful or bad-tempered personality.'

Bill scowled. 'Like that?' he asked.

'The way you're going,' said Ruth Mackenzie, 'you'll be able to take over from me any time.'

'You're a good teacher.'

'I never reject undeserved praise,' she responded quickly.

There was a long pause. 'Did you say you were free for dinner?' Bill asked.

MS CONSULTANTS
TRAINING PROGRAMME NO. 3

CANDIDATE: NEW HEAD OF PUBLIC AFFAIRS FOR A MAJOR OIL COMPANY

CONFIDENTIAL BACKGROUND REPORT

Given the new North Sea exploration plans of the Company, the new appointee is fully alert to the difficulties of the job, confronted as she is bound to be by attacks and campaigns orchestrated by Greenpeace and other environmental pressure groups. She is aware that oil companies have traditionally had to take a defensive stand on this and other fronts, with both the media and their customer base, which are always only too ready to attack them and their corporate strategies.

REPORT

The new Head of Public Affairs has been well chosen. She is bright and well turned out without being too glitzy or attractive. In our view a woman in such a position has a positive advantage. She has come from a background in environmentally friendly industries and has an alert awareness of the problems she is likely to face. Her professional qualifications are excellent. In personal projection terms, however, she is a bit strident, even screechy, particularly when she was subjected to hostile questions in our study sessions. She needs to relax and concentrate on what she and the Company want to make known, and to avoid always being pushed on to the defensive. The Company has a good, considerate profile with the country at large. She needs to harness and build on that and to be seen not as aggressive and antagonistic, nor as apologetic when under threat. She needs to be the voice of reason. She should also attempt to lower her voice pitch and tone and choose her clothes with care, so as to be seen as very environmentally aware, rather than someone carrying lots of metropolitan chic.

RESULTS

At first she was naturally defensive over both her voice and appearance, but we persuaded her that what we were talking about were tiny changes of emphasis and style rather than anything dramatic. We did not mean to change her into something she is not. She is now fully aware, having watched numerous clips of television interviews with the spokesmen for various environmental lobby groups, that she must not contrast too much with them, for example through power dressing or by using over-authoritative, London-based voice tones.

CHAPTER 10

Hearing from the Experts

Going for professional advice

The populace, in choosing between candidates, relies on common gossip and on their reputation, when it has otherwise no knowledge of them based on noteworthy deeds; or else on some preconceived opinion it has formed of them.

Machiavelli

For the great majority of mankind are satisfied with appearances, as though they were realities, and are often more influenced by the things that *seem* than by those that *are*.

Machiavelli

Fortune is the arbiter of half the things we do, leaving the other half to be controlled by ourselves.

Machiavelli

Spin-doctoring and public relations get a bad press. Harold Wilson called the latter 'organized lying'. Yet we live in a mass communications world where what we see is what we make judgements on. What do we really know about what most public figures are like? We hang on the lips of lawyers, doctors and bankers. We do what they advise, though we have little or no in-depth knowledge of their skills. It is important to us that people like them not only look reassuring but communicate accurately and effectively. It is only sensible, whatever we ourselves do, to take professional advice about improving how we too are seen and how we communicate at work and at leisure.

This is the age of the spin-doctor. I first came across the term in the United States way back in the mid-seventies, but it was not in common use in the United Kingdom until relatively recently. Now hardly a day goes by without commentators on radio or television pontificating on this or that aspect of the 'spin' put on the public presentation of current events.

What do such professional image consultants and trainers do? First of all, if they are wise, they do not try to make any fundamental change in their client. That almost never works. Remember how the image merchants tried to work over Neil Kinnock, suddenly putting him into well-cut shirts and double-breasted pinstripe suits? It was all too late, and the boyo image stayed with us despite all these later attempts at window-dressing him. What the experts can do, if they are good at their job, is to identify and build on the good points of someone and reduce or eliminate the bad, *before* their client hits the headlines. Unless they work on what exists, or unless the client is a supreme actor, the empty shell will be exposed all too quickly.

Your first step, if you decide to take outside advice, is to set about deciding from whom to seek it. As I said earlier, the danger with family and friends is that they come along with a lot of inherited emotional baggage and experience of you, and their consequent ability to see what sort of Primacy Effect you have on others will be as warped and blinkered as your own. That is why skilled professional outside image consultants are of much more use. Even honest working colleagues will avoid telling you some giant home truth. Additionally, their familiarity with you, if it does not always breed contempt, does tend to lessen the aura of your skills somewhat, on the lines of a prophet being without honour in his own country. We see this with public figures who, once remote, are now seen daily and in close-up on our television screens, warts and all.

Having made your choice, you have to place a lot of trust in your spin-doctor if he or she is to be of any real use in changing your marketability in life. Some people tend to deride such image building and those who undertake it, whether as client or teacher. They are often the people who think this sort of thing does not matter. They are incapable of understanding their own negative image. Take the example of the former Home Secretary, Michael Howard. An intelligent and pleasant man in private, his public face was his undoing. He was immaculate in everything except his ability to convince, and was incapable of persuading the public, and even most of his party, to appreciate his merits and those of the policies he was advocating. In

Physician – heal thyself !

the end he had everyone – judges, lawyers, police, civil servants, even the prison population – against him. He proved that to be successful, and not only in political life, one has to have both popular views and a popular personality. People do not follow detailed arguments, particularly on radio and television. They ask instead: is this an agreeable or a nasty person talking to me in my living room? Mr Howard, for all his qualities and for all the belated efforts of his handlers, failed that most basic test. He did not have what it takes.

Charisma

What does it take to be able to persuade and convince if you are in public life? What of the Primacy Effect on the national stage? This raises the whole question of what is sometimes called charisma and its various bedfellows. Words bandied about in the media include *gravitas, substance, hinterland, bottom* and *natural authority*, with the interrelationships among leaders and between them and the people expressed by words like personal chemistry or rapport. Charisma is much discussed when, for example, television pundits and others try to define the keys to winning an election. The personalities of the politicians involved are more studied than their policies: who is doing the talking is always more interesting than what is being said.

Charisma has always been an extremely hard concept to define. All we can be sure of is that very few people have had it. We would never call Margaret Thatcher charismatic, though on the world stage Nelson Mandela and John F. Kennedy were both public figures who were seen to have this particular attribute. Charisma goes way beyond even inspired leadership. It includes something emotionally charging in the make-up of the person who has it. Looking around at the world's religious leaders for examples of authority and of the position investing the holder of it with a special dignity, the Pope, the Dalai Lama and the Aga Khan will have less effect on most of the rest of the world than they do on their immediate followers. The Revd Dr Billy Graham, by contrast, with his unique evangelical style, enthused millions throughout the world in a long and distinguished career. The present Pope is not a demonstrative man, but his sincerity patently demonstrates his faith, while the Dalai Lama, frequently pictured with a

By your aura are you known

light shining around his head by carefully chosen photographs, has a worldwide reputation as much for the freedoms he stands for as for what he is.

Some people seem to make a virtue of the fact that they are not particularly charismatic or exciting to know. Sir Peter Davis, the head of the UK's Prudential Assurance Company, himself appears widely on radio and television as 'The Man from the Pru'. Straightforward, honest, bespectacled and plump, he is very much like lots of people we all know in day-to-day life, unglamorous but trustworthy and sensible.

There are other people of considerable prominence and financial power to whom a public image not only does not seem to matter, but who actively avoid creating one. The secretive and reclusive twins, the Barclay Brothers, who own, among other things, London's Ritz Hotel, the *European* magazine and the *Scotsman* publications, are cases in point. They have almost never been photographed and spend their time safeguarding their privacy in the South of France or on a remote private retreat in the Channel Islands. By the very determined nature of their modesty they have created a myth for the headline writers.

Some of the greatest names in world trade and industry also carry with them an aura of mystery. We know what we have read about Lord Hanson or Tiny Rowland or the billionaire trader George Soros, or someone like Rupert Murdoch. But what are they like in real life? A lot of people had views on the late Robert Maxwell and found him difficult if not odious to deal with, but it wasn't until after his death that the true nature of the man and the reality of his financial chicaneries were at last revealed. So it is with lesser people. If at the top of the industrial tree so little is known about people except what is seen in the public domain, the rest of us can hardly expect to fare differently. The world is full of people who have climbed to the top and gained huge publicity without much due cause. The millionaire developer and celebrity Donald Trump is a superb example of someone who, without his tempestuous social life and the fact that he has had a number of widely reported marriages, not least with the renowned Ivana, would doubtless be just another big business man. He is of the type that *Hello!* magazine caters for in its profiles. These people are famous for being famous.

It also frequently happens in the world of showbusiness and of fashion that reputations are made by outrageously and very deliberately overstepping the mark. Vivienne Westwood sets out to shock the public with her see-through dresses, while Alexander McQueen becomes the talk of the fashion world when it is rumoured that one of his collections for Givenchy contains human body parts. A number of artists like Damien Hirst – he of the pickled sheep – only reach the headlines because they set out to offend by producing what most members of the public believe to be spurious 'works of art'. In a much more reasonable way Richard Branson, with his huge aptitude for self-publicity, deliberately sets out to attract coverage by means of stunts, as when he shaved off his beard and dressed up in a bride's outfit to promote some new venture. He hit the headlines in a way that most captains of industry would never seek to do.

Such personal traits in public individuals are what appeal or repel. People do make judgements about their would-be overlords in terms of what they think of their integrity, their honesty, their likeability – but in a recent poll conducted to discover the most essential attribute of all, that word charisma came a close second to leadership. Mere competence tended to have a lower placing, along with such other difficult attributes to define as charm and energy. During an election campaign, especially a long one like the 1997 General Election, the huge amount of media exposure which the various party leaders were given by the media was a huge turn-off in the eyes of most television viewers. In all walks of life, familiarity does tend eventually to breed some contempt, which reminds us of the age-old saying that no great leader is a hero in the eyes of his valet.

Office and Authority

The holding of some great 'office', followed by the eventual leaving of it, shows up the personal impact skills of once-important individuals in particularly naked relief. Men and women are listened to with attention when they hold important appointments. Rank dresses them large. But most of them, even the Ronald Reagans and the Margaret Thatchers of the world, are diminished, made tawdry, almost comic at times, when they leave centre-stage. The trappings of power, once stripped away, can show the comparative insignificance of the human being beneath, thus proving Talleyrand's percipient remark that 'nations would be terrified if they knew by what small men they are governed'. Without the oxygen of publicity, they disappear.

Some people, however, when they leave centre-stage, have a continuing shelf-life for years to come. In the best Eisenhower tradition, America likes its military men. People like General Colin Powell and Stormin' Norman Schwarzkopf, that great bull of a military leader, still retain their positions of respect in the American public hierarchy long after they have demitted office. It would not surprise anyone if General Powell, in particular, runs for presidential office in the not too distant future, based on the reputation he made on the field of battle. The shelf-life of certain great individuals often outlasts even their deaths, as we know from Elvis Presley, who through the marvels of marketing has a name worth more now than when he died way back in 1977. Other reputations, once established, change over the years, as with that sad but once great figure, now suffering from Parkinson's Disease, Muhammad Ali.

In Britain, whether we like him or not, Sir Edward Heath has remained on public view because he has decided to sit it out on the benches of the House of Commons. Other of his contemporaries, like Lord (Jim) Callaghan, disappeared into the House of Lords, as doubtless will most members of John Major's former Tory cabinet. The game of 'Where Are They Now?' is one that is played not only in political life but also in industry and commerce, where the captains and the kings of British industrial life mainly vanish the very moment they demit office. Only a few, like the former head of ICI, John Harvey-Jones, deliberately decide to move into other fields of activity which bring them as much, if not more, popularity and acclaim. Then there are a number of people in life who are famous or notorious only for being famous. They are of the Liz Hurley variety, the actress known for having been a girlfriend of Hugh Grant, and for having worn revealing dresses on showbiz occasions. The tabloids and the gossip columns are littered with socialites or 'It Girls' with names like Tara Palmer Tomkinson, or Tamara Beckwith, who have absolutely no reason for having a reputation other than having a reputation.

Now back to *your* reputation. I quoted a lot of Machiavelli at the beginning of this chapter. Here is another pertinent thought from him:

> A prince who is not himself wise cannot be well advised unless he puts himself in the hands of one individual who looks after his affairs and is extremely shrewd.

What you need from your image trainer is the truth, not flattery. Even sharp-tongued colleagues and your most critical friends are bad at proffering the former.

Spin-doctoring for Beginners

So sit back and think very carefully. Whom do *you* listen to? Whom do you *really* listen to? Whose advice, wisdom, judgement and strategic thinking and so on do you admire, respect and follow? At a guess, you'll agree there are few around. A danger to watch for here is that the higher up any ladder you go, the more flatterers there are to court you. You have seen it yourself: particularly with weak managers in a business, sycophants rule. To such hangers-on, having a good personal relationship with their boss becomes an end in itself, with other much more important objectives taking second place. Such a situation develops where a Chief Executive has become a victim of his or her own success. They believe in their own right to rule and are helped in the fantasy by the yes-men or women who tell them only what they want to hear. We all need to watch for this: we need honest feedback and constructive criticism rather than answers that are proffered only because they are acceptable.

Somebody once said, 'Nothing succeeds like reputation', and a good image consultant or spin-doctor will start off by looking very closely at what you want from them. They won't want to upstage you, getting between you and the footlights, but will try to build for you a status and reputation that is going to be useful to you in the years ahead. It is not a matter of bolstering some false image of you, but getting the most positive one seen by the outside world. Of course, there are some major business leaders who don't need or want and would never take such advice. I have worked with many extremely able business people who are poor communicators, yet who don't give a fig for their image, do not ever wish to speak publicly, and are happy to be protected from the media and from the outside world by the company spokesman in the PR Department. If that is your style, then I would certainly not suggest that you force yourself to change it if that would make you unhappy.

British spin-doctors, following the American example, boldly talk about, 'selling the Prime Minister' or creating a high-profile image for some new CEO, which demeans what is a perfectly natural thing to do in business or public life – making sure the best and most helpful message about you and your organization gets through to your various audiences. You need help in specific situations that you meet, particularly when you have been promoted into some senior position and outsiders start to notice you whether you like it or not. You are also going to need advice when things are tough or are in danger of going wrong.

Many such personal PR exercises are a waste of time and money. Those who rely heavily on poor advisers in this field are in constant danger of being exposed. As a senior manager or business leader, you have got to be very clear about what *you* want, and to remain in full charge. You don't need someone who is going to do something clever themselves. You want them to advise *you* how *you* should do it, otherwise it can go wrong. An example of such PR overshadowing reality took place in the summer of 1997, when British Airways launched its new international hotchpotch of an image, dropping the Union Jack from the tailfins of its aircraft and so on. On the back of this move, much criticized by the media, what did Richard Branson and Virgin Airways do but immediately announce that in future the Virgin logo on their aircraft would proudly incorporate the flag! At minimal cost, he got massive plaudits at the expense of British Airways, which went away to lick its corporate wounds.

Life Coaching

That is all big business. What lessons does it have for you? What about your personal logo? Looking at things in this totally different way is the basis of the new American concept of 'Life Coaching'. Life coaches train an increasing number of high flyers in the United States. Such training also exists in Britain, though it is called by a variety of other less glamorous names, and individuals usually only go to such career advisers when they are out of a job and looking to outplace themselves in some other direction.

Before you deride the whole life coach idea, however, pause for a moment. There is a lot going for it. A life coach, like a professional personal impact adviser or someone who helps you hone up your Primacy Effect – call them what you will – can be a positive figure in helping you realize your full personal and professional potential. These are trained specialists who don't beat about the bush but get to the real issues. They ask:

- 'Are you really happy with what you're doing now and your current level of achievement?'
- 'Do you want a change?'
- 'Why do you want to change?'
- 'What have you done recently which will help you to change?'
- 'How are you going to set about it?'

These and other fundamental questions force you to concentrate your mind. Of course, many of us are perfectly capable of doing all this for ourselves. We don't need outside help. Others, often quite successful people, are not so fortunate. So if you want a fairly aggressive and intrusive push to where you want to go, a life coach or personal spin-doctor can play the role of part guru, part therapist, part friend, in helping you plan your future business and private life.

An adviser will want to know as many details of your lifestyle as a personal fitness trainer. Are you eating, sleeping and exercising effectively? They will want to know whether you have any money worries, sexual problems or other anxieties which are going to intrude into your general feeling of well-being. Life coaches are not psychologists or shrinks, yet they too will need to examine every aspect of your life, from the fact that you have been putting off going to the dentist to anxieties over how the next gas bill is going to be met. Such personal coaches build up a close personal partnership which can be fraught with dangers if you don't have the right person. If you have a tennis coach, you can walk away when you are not playing tennis. If you have a life coach, he or she will get involved in every aspect of everything you do, and so I certainly would not advocate bringing such a person into your life without a lot of thought. But the basic idea is a useful one, as getting professional advice generally is.

Psychologists spend a lot of time rooting into your subconscious to find out what things in your childhood set you on the road you are on today. Critical to this is a realization that unless you have your private life in some sort of order it is going to spill over into your business life and you are going to find it much more difficult to cope with the day-to-day problems that face you. Impartial personal advisers will be firm, frank and fierce if need be, to get you moving in the right direction, ridding you of the negative aspects of your Primacy Effect. Life coaching goes beyond all this. Some will take on everything, telling you when to ditch a job and even when to ditch your boyfriend or girlfriend. In America they take it all one stage further: good life coaches have their own life coaches. In Britain we are still some way away from all that. But do not let us mock. Professional guides are paid to tell you the hard bits: how to stand, speak, dress, exude confidence, interview well and so on. Like it or not, it's a growing profession. All of us need impartial advice sometimes, just as we need it in financial and physical health matters. We need it to tell us where we are going, what we want out of life, and how to get there. We need it, above all, to tell us how to get our Primacy Effect right, because without that, nothing else is going to click into shape.

'Are you offering to be my personal coach?' asked Bill.

'We've got beyond that stage.' said Ruth Mackenzie. 'You've been a good pupil.'

'Grateful'. Bill stared hard at her.

'There are a few things I could improve still.' She stared back at him.

'What had you in mind?'

'Still a bit brash and brusque, but I suppose that's your style. But there's another reason why I wouldn't do it.'

'Why?' asked Bill.

'The best spin-doctors are the ones that aren't noticed. The entire office knows what I've been doing here, and if you and I were to be seen together too much – well, they might draw the wrong conclusions.'

'I overheard two secretaries whispering the other day. I think they've drawn a wrong conclusion already.'

'What could you possibly mean?' asked Ruth Mackenzie with a shy smile.

CHAPTER 11

Where Do We Go From Here?

The basic bullets

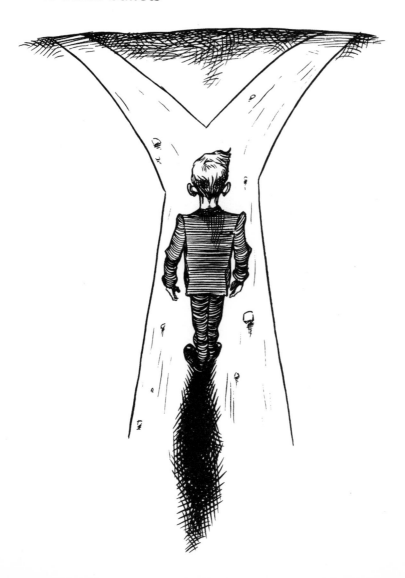

We are all in the gutter, but some of us are looking at the stars.

Oscar Wilde

Speech is the index of the mind.

Seneca

Authority is not authoritarian, nor gravitas grave, nor charisma charismatic.

Michael Sinclair

There are only two qualities in the world: efficiency and inefficiency;
and only two sorts of people: the efficient and the inefficient.

George Bernard Shaw

All of us, most of the time, have to relate to the outside world and the people in it. While some of us can and do achieve inner contentment and fulfilment, our *lifeweb*, that pattern and the satisfaction we gain from our relationships, is crucial to normal happiness. Other people make life bearable or unbearable, heaven or hell, and many degrees in between.

Our Primacy Effect and all that goes with it, can make all the difference both to this and to the other ambitions of our lives. This is neither fad nor fantasy. This is the clever truth.

When we interact with people, we try to make sense of their actions and anticipate what they may or may not do in the future. We then adjust our own actions accordingly. They, equally, in deciding whether to select us as friend or colleague or to fulfil some high task or position, will try to gauge and predict our abilities and our reactions in any given set of circumstances. Both we and they winnow out a huge amount of extraneous information which only confuses the issue. We and they concentrate on areas of perceived certainty, judging each other even though there is no conclusive proof that we or they are up to that image. We all grow into the reputation we have.

Frequently, if we 'want' someone enough, for whatever purpose, we will deliberately ignore the downside aspects of their character because we feel that such weaknesses are outweighed by the positive strengths involved. Once again we have to make absolutely certain that our plus points, from the very outset, are clearly and unambiguously stated.

Here, with no apologies for the repetition, is a checklist of what you need to watch.

1. *Self assessment*
- Is it an honest assessment?
- Are you sure?
- How can you check/find out?
- Whom are you going to ask?
- Can you trust that assessor?
- Now that you know, what are you going to do about it?

2. Action plan

Remember:

- The 50/40/10 communication breakdown
- That perception is reality
- The fifteen-second rule
- To use a mirror with memory
- To prepare an Action Dossier
- The twenty interview answers regime
- That posture, not posturing, is the solution
- That the Primacy Effect is crucial.

3. Who are you talking to? Who is your real audience?

- What do they want?
- Why should they listen?
- How can you establish a Perceived Community of Interest?
- Are you going in at the right level?
- Are you going in at the right time and place?
- How are you going to plug your unique selling point/core strengths?
- Are you sure you know the *zeitgeist* – their needs and what's needed?

4. What is your precise strategy?

Do you:

- Know your subject?
- Know your territory?
- Know your message?

Are you ready to:

- Enter the arena with that necessary ring of confidence?
- Give responses, not answers that can leave key strengths unstated?

Have you:

- Trained/rehearsed/trained/rehearsed?
- Developed the strategy, 'You have a problem, I am your solution'?

5. Basic principles

- Keep it brief.
- Don't be led astray. Keep to your key points.
- Keep good eye-contact.
- Sit up/be sharp.
- Train/rehearse/train/rehearse.
- Assess the competition.

- Slot in one key/astute remark that sticks.
- Watch your body language.
- And your paralanguage.
- Remember that image and perception outlast reality.
- Above all, remember *the Primacy Effect*.

APPENDIX

As I was finishing this book, by chance I read the following section from Shakespeare's *Hamlet*, Act III, Scene ii, where Hamlet himself is explaining to the strolling players how to act the play about his father's murder. It proves the genius of the man, and that, in the field of personal impact and the Primacy Effect, there is little new under the sun. It is well worth reading carefully and in full. 'Groundlings', you will remember, were the common people who stood and watched the play from the pit!

Hamlet:
Speak the speech, I pray you, as I pronounced it to you, trippingly on the tongue; but if you mouth it, as many of your players do, I had as lief the town-crier spoke my lines. Nor do not saw the air too much with your hand thus; but use all gently: for in the very torrent, tempest, and – as I may say – whirlwind of your passion, you must acquire and beget a temperance that may give it smoothness. O! It offends me to the soul to hear a robustious periwig-pated fellow tear a passion to tatters, to very rags, to split the ears of the groundlings, who for the most part are capable of nothing but inexplicable dumb shows and noise. I would have such a fellow whipp'd for o'erdoing Termagant; it out-herods Herod: pray you avoid it.

Be not too tame neither, but let you own discretion be your tutor: suit the action to the word, the word to the action; with this special observance, that you o'erstep not the modesty of nature ... The purpose of playing, whose end, both at the first and now, was and is to hold, as 'twere, the mirror up to nature.

INDEX